*Presents*

# GUITAR
## MASTER EDITION

# A COMPLETE COURSE FOR PLAYING GUITAR

**Supervising Editor:** John McCarthy
**Music Transcribing & Engraving:** Jimmy Rutkowski
**Production Manager:** John McCarthy
**Layout, Graphics & Design:** Jimmy Rutkowski

**Copy Editor:** Cathy McCarthy

**Cover Art Direction & Design:**
Jimmy Rutkowski

HL233444
ISBN: 978-1-4950-9357-9
Produced by John McCarthy®

# Table Of Contents

Even though the future seems far away,
it is actually beginning right now.

~ Mattie Stepanek ~

# Digital eBook

When you register this product at the lesson support site RockHouseMethod.com, you will receive a digital version of this book. This interactive eBook can be used on all devices that support Adobe PDF. This will allow you to access your book using the latest portable technology any time you want.

# Icon Key

These tell you there is additional information and learning utilities available at RockHouseMethod.com to support that lesson.

## Backing Track

Backing track icons are placed on lessons where there is an audio demonstration to let you hear what that lesson should sound like or a backing track to play the lesson over. Use these audio tracks to guide you through the lessons. **Use your member number to register at the *Lesson Support* site and download the corresponding audio tracks.**

## Metronome

Metronome icons are placed next to the examples that we recommend you practice using a metronome. You can download a free, adjustable metronome on the *Lesson Support* site.

## Worksheet

Worksheets are a great tool to help you thoroughly learn and understand music. These worksheets can be downloaded at the *Lesson Support* site.

## Tuner

You can download the free online tuner on the *Lesson Support* site to help tune your instrument.

# Parts of The Guitar

The guitar is divided into three main sections: the body, the neck and the headstock. The assembly that anchors the strings to the body is called the bridge. The bridge pins are the string pegs that secure the strings to the bridge, and the saddle holds them properly in place. On many guitars, the height of the strings (or action) can be adjusted using the saddle. The sound hole on the body projects the sound from the guitar. Some guitars also have a pick guard to protect the wood from getting scratched by the pick. At the end of the body is the strap button where a guitar strap can be attached. The front face of the neck is called the fretboard (or fingerboard). The metal bars going across the fretboard are called frets. The dots are position markers (or fret markers) for visual reference to help you gauge where you are on the neck while playing. The nut is the string guide that holds the strings in place where the neck meets the headstock. The headstock contains the machine heads (also referred to as tuners); the machine heads are used to tune the strings by tightening or loosening them.

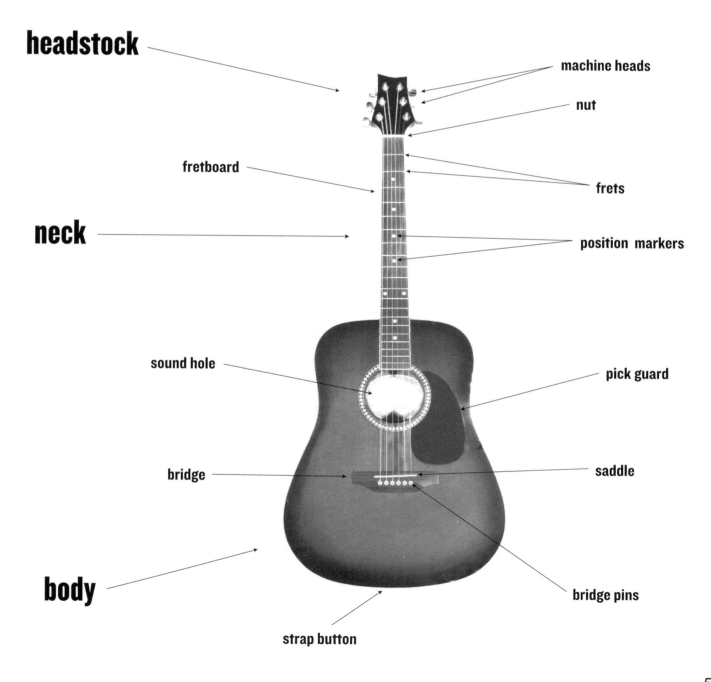

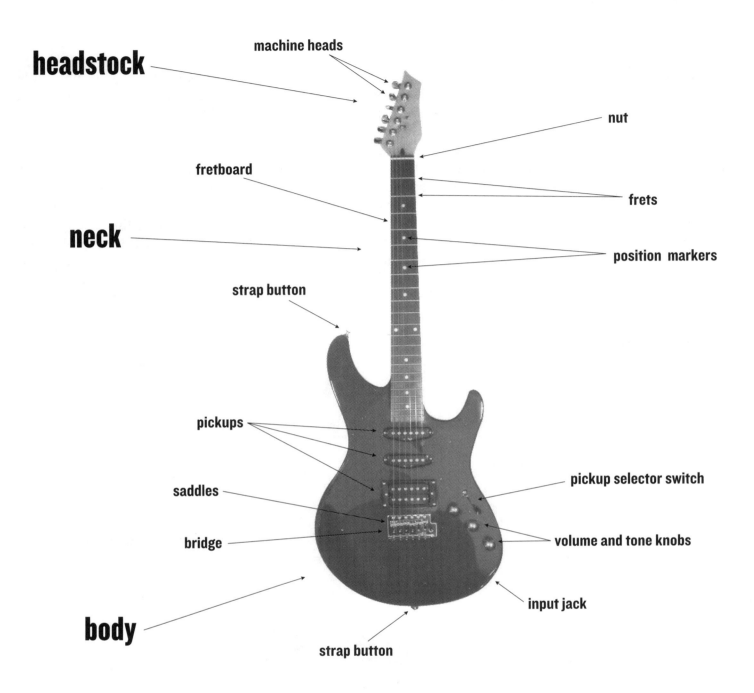

**headstock**

machine heads

nut

fretboard

frets

**neck**

position markers

strap button

pickups

pickup selector switch

saddles

bridge

volume and tone knobs

input jack

**body**

strap button

## Quick Quote!

"Rock & Roll is the physical thing that just comes out of you...the other stuff you have to sit down and learn...once you learn scales and chord progressions, you can make up your own versions."

- Brian Setzer

# Holding the Guitar

The photos below show the proper way to hold a guitar. You can rest the body of the guitar on your right or left leg - either way is correct. Certain styles of music may be played more comfortably one way or the other. Experiment with it and decide which way feels more natural.

Throughout this book we will refer to the picking hand as your right hand and the hand fretting the notes as your left hand. If you are left handed and playing a left handed guitar, just make the necessary adjustments as you follow along (read "right hand" to mean your left hand and vice versa).

## Holding the Pick

The photos below show the proper way to hold a guitar. You can rest the body of the guitar on your right or left leg - either way is correct. Certain styles of music may be played more comfortably one way or the other. Experiment with it and decide which way feels more natural.

Throughout this book we will refer to the picking hand as your right hand and the hand fretting the notes as your left hand. If you are left handed and playing a left handed guitar, just make the necessary adjustments as you follow along (read "right hand" to mean your left hand and vice versa).

Grasp the pick between your index finger and thumb.

Leave your hand open and your other fingers loose.

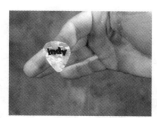
Fig. 1

Fig. 2

Fig. 3

To properly position the pick, center the pick on your index finger **(Fig. 1)** and bring your thumb down on top of it **(Fig. 2)**. Pinch your thumb and finger together and leave just the tip of the pick showing **(Fig. 3)**.

# Right Hand Position

Place your right arm on the very top of the guitar and let it drape down almost parallel to the bridge **(Fig. 4)**. Leave part of your hand or fingers touching the guitar's body and keep them anchored to the guitar **(Fig. 5)**. This will help give your picking hand a reference point.

Fig. 4

Fig. 5

# Right Hand Position

Hold your left hand out in front of you with your wrist straight (Fig. 6). Curl your fingers in and just naturally bring your hand back to the neck of the guitar (Figs. 7 & 8). Try not to bend or contort your wrist. Your fingers should stay curled inward; most of the time only your fingertips will touch the strings when playing. The first joint of your thumb should be in the middle of the back of the neck (Fig. 9). Try to avoid touching the neck with any other part of your hand. Make sure you have the proper right and left hand positions down so that when we progress you'll have no problems.

Rest the guitar on your right leg when seated.

When standing, the guitar strap goes over your left shoulder.

Be sure the amplifier is turned off before you plug in.

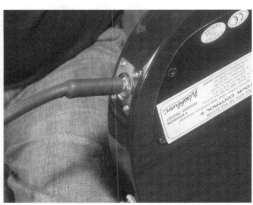
Insert the cord all the way into the input jack.

# Tuning

Each of the six strings on a guitar is tuned to and named after a different note (pitch). The thinnest or 1st string is referred to as the highest string because it is the highest sounding string. The thickest or 6th string is referred to as the lowest string because it is the lowest sounding string. Memorize the names of the open strings. These notes form the basis for finding any other notes on the guitar.

| 6th string | 5th string | 4th string | 3rd string | 2nd string | 1st string |
|:---:|:---:|:---:|:---:|:---:|:---:|
| E | A | D | G | B | E |

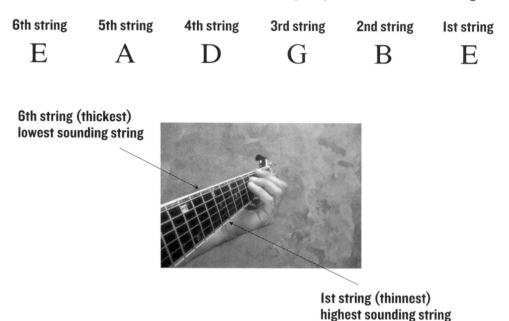

6th string (thickest)
lowest sounding string

1st string (thinnest)
highest sounding string

Tune your guitar using the machine heads on the headstock. Turn the machine heads a little bit at a time while plucking the string and listening to the change in pitch. Tighten the string to raise the pitch. Loosen the string to lower the pitch. Be careful not to accidentally break a string by tightening it too much or too quickly.

The easiest way to tune a guitar is to use an electronic tuner. There are many different kinds available that are fairly inexpensive. You can also download the free online tuner from **www.rockhousemethod.com**.

# Reading a Chord Chart

A chord is a group of notes played together. A chord chart (chord diagram) is a graphic representation of part of the fretboard (as if you stood the guitar up from floor to ceiling and looked directly at the front of the neck). The vertical lines represent the strings; the horizontal lines represent the frets.

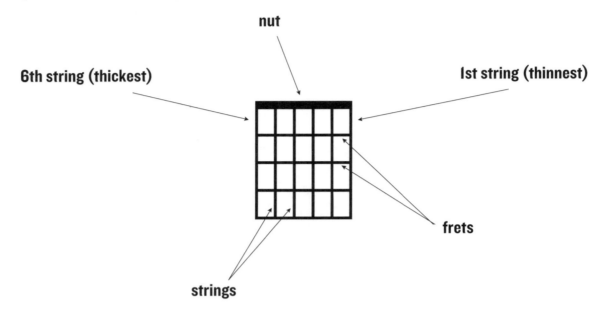

Chord diagrams show which notes to play and which strings they are played on. The solid black dots within the graph represent fretted notes and show you where your fingers should go. Each of these dots will have a number directly below it, underneath the diagram. These numbers indicate which left hand finger to fret the note with (1 = index, 2 = middle, 3 = ring, 4 = pinky). The 0s at the bottom of the diagram show which strings are played open (strummed with no left hand fingers touching them).

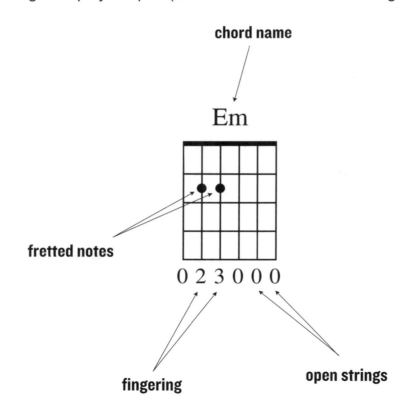

10

# Your First Chords

Our first two chords are two of the easiest and most commonly used chords in rock and blues, A minor and E minor. In the Am chord diagram, the "x" at the 6th string means that string is not played (either muted or not strummed). For each chord, the first photo shows what the chord looks like from the front. The second photo is from the player's perspective. Minor chords are represented in this book using a capital letter, which refers to the letter name of the chord, followed by a lowercase "m" indicating that the chord is a minor chord.

Am

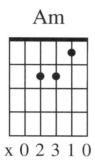

x 0 2 3 1 0

Em

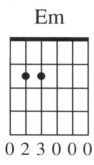

0 2 3 0 0 0

Remember to keep your thumb firmly anchored against the back of the neck. Your fingers should be curled inward toward the fretboard and only the tips of your fingers should be touching the strings. Don't grab the neck with your whole hand; no other parts of your fingers or hand should be touching the neck or any of the other strings. Place your fingertips just to the left of (behind) the fret, pressing the strings inward toward the neck.

Let's start off with a simple down strum. Fret the Am chord with your left hand. Starting from the 5th string, lightly drag the pick downward across the strings in a smooth motion. Now switch to the Em chord and strum downward from the 6th (thickest) string. The strumming motion should come from your elbow and wrist. When strumming chords, pivot from your elbow and keep your wrist straight. When playing single notes, use more wrist.

One of the hardest things for a beginner to conquer is the ability to play a clean, fully sustained chord without buzzing strings, muted or dead notes. Make sure your left hand is fretting the proper notes and your fingers aren't accidentally touching any of the other strings. Pick each string individually with your right hand, one note at a time. If any of the open strings are deadened or muted, try slightly adjusting your fingers. If any of the fretted notes are buzzing, you probably aren't pressing down hard enough with your fingers. It will be difficult at first and might hurt a little, but don't get discouraged. With time and practice, you'll build up calluses on your fingertips. Before you know it, playing chords will be second nature and your fingers will hardly feel it at all.

# Strumming Rhythm

Once you have the chords sounding clean and the strumming motion down, the next step is to learn how to change chords quickly and cleanly. Focus on where each finger needs to move for the next chord. Sometimes one or more of your fingers will be able to stay in the same place. Avoid taking your hand completely off the neck. Instead, try to move your whole hand as little as possible and make smaller finger adjustments to change from one chord to the next. When you can change from chord to chord seamlessly, you'll be able to play complete songs.

The following is an example of a chord progression and is written on a musical staff. A staff is the group of horizontal lines on which music is written. The chord names above the staff show which chord to play, and the rhythm slashes indicate the rhythm in which the chords are strummed. In this chord progression, strum each chord twice, using all down strums. This example also uses repeat signs (play through the progression and repeat it again). Listen and play along with the backing track to hear how it should sound. Keep practicing and try to change chords in time without stalling or missing a beat. Count along out loud with each strum, in time and on the beat. Start out slowly if you need to and gradually get it up to speed.

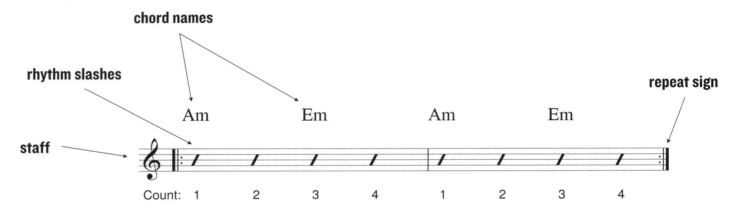

# Counting Beats

A beat is the basic unit of time in music. A common way to count beats is to tap your foot. One beat would equal tapping your foot down-up. Tap your foot and count 1 – 2 – 3 – 4 repetitively, say each number as your foot hits the ground. You will learn different note types that tell you how many beats to let notes ring.

### Foot Down

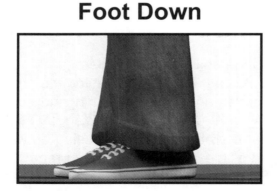

### Foot Up

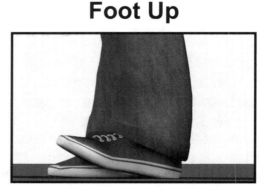

# Rhythm Notation

You don't need to read traditional music notation in order to play guitar, but it's helpful to understand a little bit about the concept of rhythm and timing. In most popular rock and blues, music is divided into measures of four beats. When a band counts off "One, two, three, four" at the beginning of a song, it represents one complete measure of music. Different types of notes are held for different durations within a measure. For example, a quarter note gets one beat because a quarter note is held for one quarter of a measure.

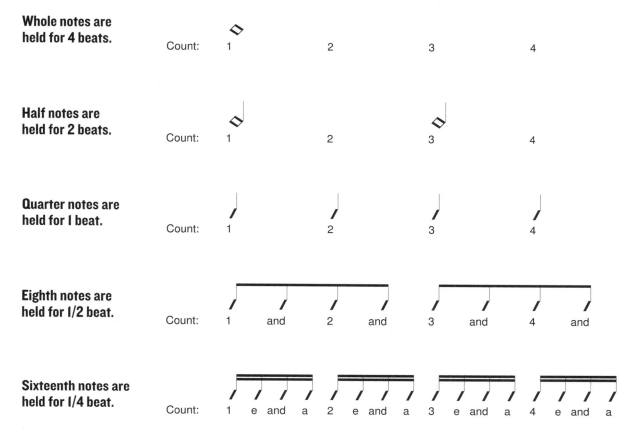

A tie is a curved line connecting one note to the next. If two notes are tied, strike only the first one and let it ring out through the duration of the second note (or "tied" note).

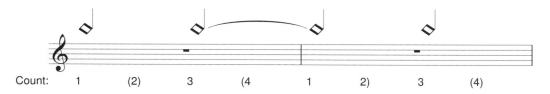

A dot after a note increases its value by another 1/2 of its original value. In the following example the half notes are dotted, so they are held for three beats.

# Major Open Chords

Now it's time to play some major chords. Major chords have a happy, royal or bright sound, whereas the minor chords have a sad or melancholy type of sound. All of the major and minor chords in this chapter are open chords because they contain open strings and are played in the first position on the fretboard. Major chords are represented in this book using a capital letter by itself for the chord name. They can also be shown using the letter name followed by a capital letter M, Maj, or Major. E, A and D are three of the easiest and most used major chords. Many blues songs can be played entirely using just these three chords. The first chord below is the E major chord.

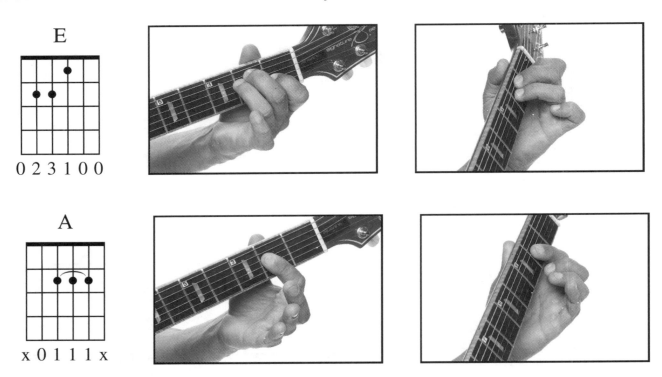

In the A chord diagram, the slur going across the notes means you should barre (bar) those notes. A barre is executed by placing one finger flat across more than one string. Pick each note of the chord individually to make sure you're applying enough pressure with your finger. Notice that the 6th and 1st strings each have an "x" below them on the diagram, indicating these strings are not played (either muted or not strummed).

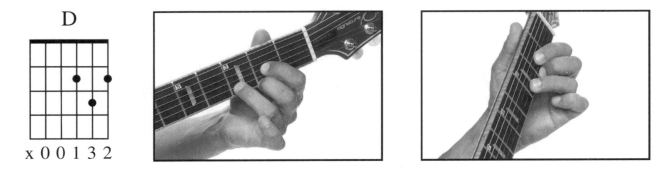

The last major open chord in this section is the D major chord. In this program the 4th and 5th strings are played open; only the 6th string is muted. Another variation of the chord you might encounter will also mute the 5th string. Adding the open 5th string as indicated below gives the chord a fuller sound.

# Picking Exercise

Here's an alternate picking exercise to help coordinate your right hand. Instead of strumming the chords, you might pick the notes of a chord out individually and let them ring out together. The following symbols indicate whether a note is picked in an up or a down direction:

⊓ - **downpick (pick down toward the floor)**

V - **uppick (pick up toward the ceiling)**

Fret an open D chord and hold the chord shape with your left hand while picking out the individual notes in the order indicated below. This picking pattern (indicated by which number string you pick) is 4 - 1 - 3 - 1 - 2 - 1. Recite the string number while you pick each one to help memorize the order. Use a down-up-down-up alternate picking pattern. Notice that the 1st string is always up picked, while the other strings are all down picked. Try to hold one of your right hand fingers on the body of the guitar to help give you added support and control. Practice playing in a steady, even rhythm, in time with a metronome.

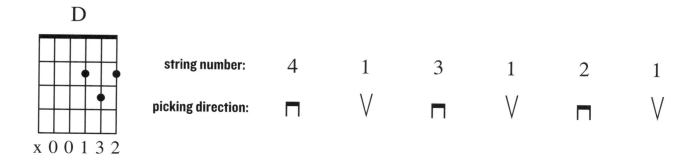

# Major Open Chord Strumming Pattern

Here's a progression using the three new chords. This example is played in an eighth note rhythm. Down strum each chord eight times. Listen to the backing track and practice changing chords cleanly and in time. You can download all of these backing tracks from the website and practice along with them.

Count: 1 and 2 and 3 and 4 and etc...

# Open Chord Blues

The following is an example of a chord progression and is written on a musical staff. A staff is the group of horizontal lines on which music is written. The chord names above the staff show which chord to play, and the rhythm slashes indicate the rhythm in which the chords are strummed. In this chord progression, strum each chord twice, using all down strums. This example also uses repeat signs (play through the progression and repeat it again). Listen and play along with the backing track to hear how it should sound. Keep practicing and try to change chords in time without stalling or missing a beat. Count along out loud with each strum, in time and on the beat. Start out slowly if you need to and gradually get it up to speed.

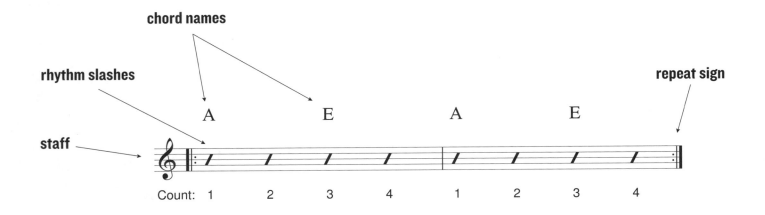

## Major Blues

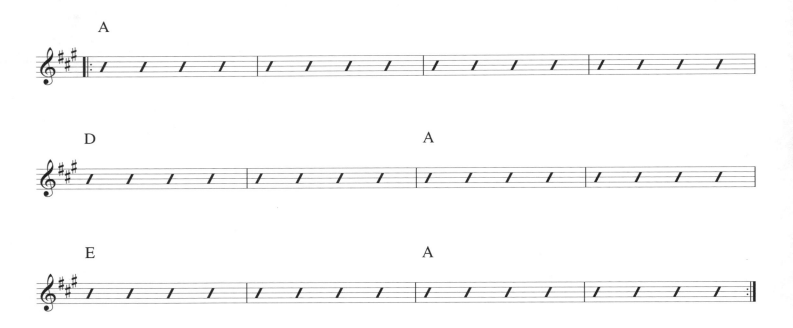

16

# Tablature Explanation

Tablature (or tab) is a number system for reading notes on the neck of a guitar. It does not require you to have knowledge of standard music notation. This system was designed specifically for the guitar. Most music for guitar is available in tab. Tablature is a crucial and essential part of your guitar playing career.

The six lines of the tablature staff represent each of the six strings. The top line is the thinnest (highest pitched) string. The bottom line is the thickest (lowest pitched) string. The lines in between are the 2nd through 5th strings. The numbers placed directly on these lines show you the fret number to play the note at. At the bottom, underneath the staff, is a series of numbers. These numbers show you which left hand fingers you should use to fret the notes.

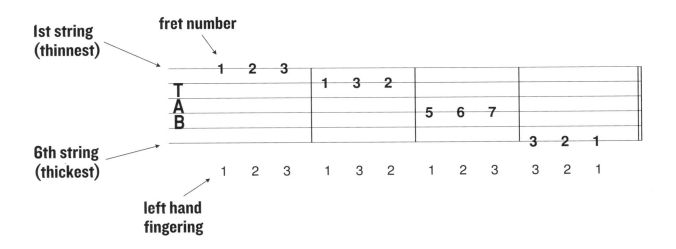

Chords can also be written in tab. If there are several numbers stacked together in a column, those notes should be played or strummed at the same time. Here are the five chords you already know from chapter 1 with the tablature written out underneath each diagram. Since the fingerings are shown on the chord diagrams, we won't bother to repeat them underneath the tab.

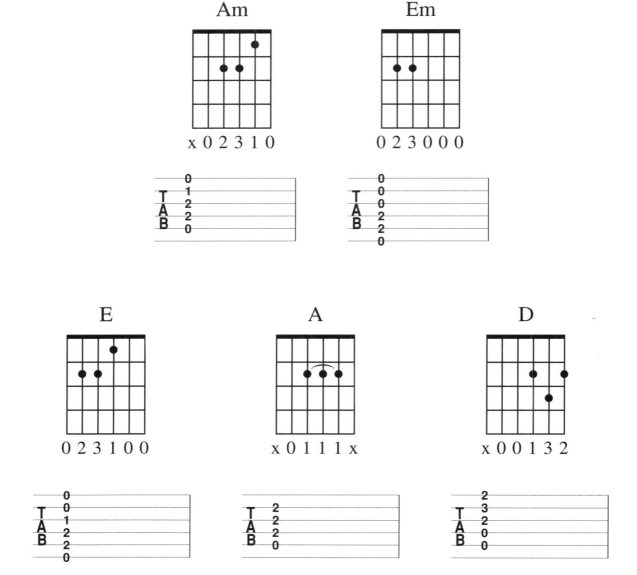

## Quick Tip!

### MAKE SURE YOUR GUITAR IS SET UP PROPERLY

*Beginners don't usually realize that their new guitar may need to be set up for it to play comfortably. A proper set up will ensure that the strings are at the correct height. If they're too high off the neck, it will be harder to press the strings down. You'll also want to check the neck adjustment to be sure your guitar neck has the proper curve. Even right out of the box, new guitars need adjusting. This oversight can cause many beginners to give up in frustration before giving it a fair chance on a properly adjusted instrument.*

# Finger Flexing Exercise

This is a finger exercise in tablature that will build coordination and strengthen your fingers. It's designed to help stretch your hand out, so keep your fingers spread across the first four frets, one finger per fret. Leave your first finger anchored in place and reach for the following three notes by stretching your hand out.

With your right hand, use alternate picking in a consistent down-up-down-up pendulum motion. Alternate picking will help develop speed, smoothness and technique. Practice this exercise using the metronome for timing and control.

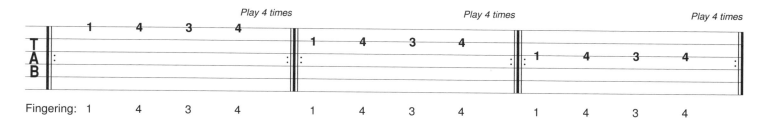

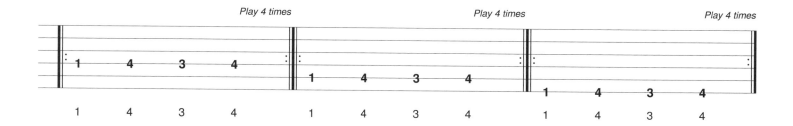

# More Major Open Chords

Four more popular major chords are B, C, F and G. The hardest one to play is the F chord. This chord is difficult to play because you need to barre the highest two strings with your first finger and put your second and third fingers down straight. If you tilt your first finger barre to the left side, it makes it easier to fret the other notes properly. Pick each note out individually to make sure the chord sounds clean and that you're playing it correctly. You should now know all seven open major chords. Practice playing them and changing from chord to chord efficiently.

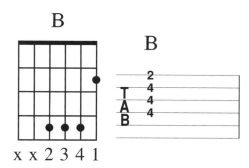

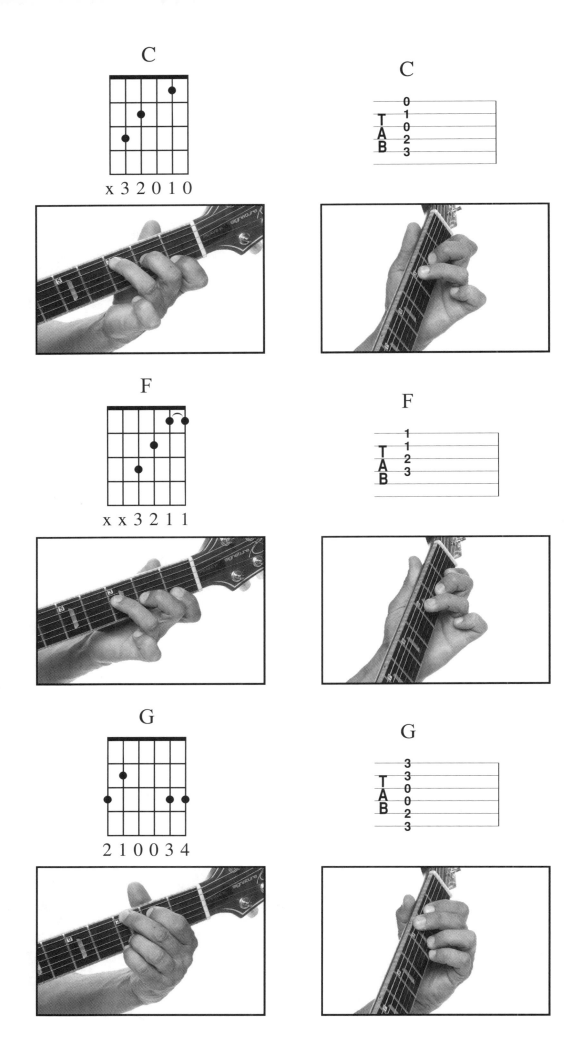

# Picking Chord Progression

Let's go through a progression that picks out the chords and combines individual picking with strumming. This is a popular two chord progression using the D and G major chords. When changing from chord to chord, notice the third finger of your left hand can stay on the same note. Leave this finger stationary when switching chords and concentrate on moving the other fingers. Follow the symbols above the staff to get the picking pattern down. Once you've got it, practice playing along with the backing track and staying in time with the bass and drums.

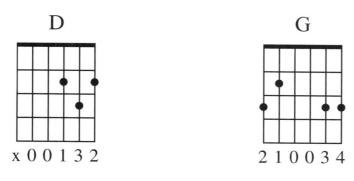

# Blues

The following is a basic blues riff in the key of A. This riff is made up of two note chords shown on the tab staff. The chord names above the staff are there as a reference to show you what the basic harmony is while you play along.

This riff should sound very familiar - it's used more than any other blues progression. Plenty of rock and blues classics are played entirely with this one riff repeated over and over. It is made up of 12 measures (or bars) of music called the 12-bar blues, a blues progression consisting of twelve repeated bars of music.

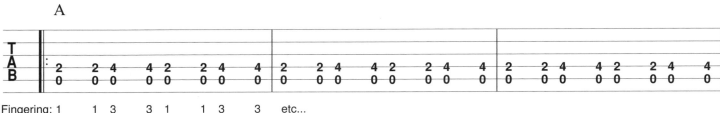

# Creating a Great Blues Sound

Effect pedals (or stomp boxes) are often used to enhance or distort a guitar's tone. There are many different types of effects. The most popular effects used for blues guitar are overdrive, distortion, chorus, delay, reverb, and wah wah. Below are a few of the most common ones. Take a trip to your local music store and try out a variety of effect pedals to hear which ones sound good to you.

## Overdrive Pedal

A distortion or overdrive pedal simulates the sound of the guitar's signal being overdriven, giving it a fuzz tone. Overdrive can be used in different degrees. Light distortion will give the sound a warm, round, or full tone. Using heavy distortion gives the guitar a heavy metal tone.

## Chorus Pedal

A chorus pedal creates the sound of a few guitars played at once. A chorus doubles the original signal with a very slight delay, causing a wavy tone that simulates a chorus of guitars.

## Wah Wah Pedal

A wah wah pedal is a foot activated pedal that you can "play" with your foot while playing the guitar. The pedal gets rocked back and forth by your foot and gives the guitar a talking, wah wah type sound. What a wah wah pedal actually does is sweep quickly back and forth between extreme bass and extreme treble driven by the movement of your foot.

## Amplifier Gain

Turning up the gain knob on an amplifier overdrives the signal and creates distortion. Use small amounts of gain for a warm, thick tone. Using high gain will cause heavy distortion. Use the gain in conjunction with the amplifier's master volume control to set the desired tone and level of the sound.

# More Minor Chords

Now let's play a few more minor chords, Bm, Cm, and Dm. Notice that the Bm and Cm chords both have the exact same fingering. To go from the Bm to the Cm, simply slide your hand up the neck one fret.

### Bm

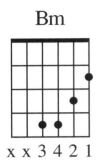

x x 3 4 2 1

### Bm

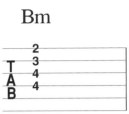

```
      2
      3
T     4
A     4
B
```

### Cm

3fr

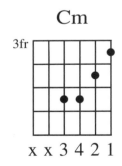

x x 3 4 2 1

### Cm

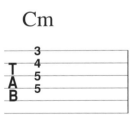

```
      3
      4
T     5
A     5
B
```

Dm

x 0 0 2 3 1

Dm

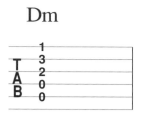

# Alternate Strumming

Up until now, we've only been using down strums. Here's a popular strumming rhythm that combines both up and down strumming. Play the chords above the staff in the rhythm and strumming pattern indicated. When alternate strumming, keep your arm relaxed and don't grip the pick too tightly. Stay nice and loose so that your strumming sounds smooth, not stiff or forced.

This progression combines both major and minor chords. When changing chords, look for common notes from one chord to the next one; don't move any fingers that can remain on the same notes.

⊓ - **downstrum (strum down toward the floor)**

∨ - **upstrum (strum up toward the ceiling)**

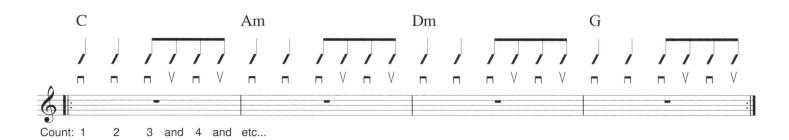

# Minor Chord Progression

Here's a popular strumming rhythm that combines both up and down strumming, as well as major and minor chords. The rhythm used is an example of syncopation. You're playing a syncopated rhythm if there are one or more strums off the beat, or on the upbeat instead of the downbeat. The strum on beat 2 1/2 is tied to beat 3, so you don't strum directly on beat 3. Keep your arm moving in a consistent down-up-down-up motion, with a ghost strum occurring on beat 3. Once you have the chord changes and strumming fluent, use the CD or download the backing track from the Rock House Lesson Support site and practice playing along with the bass and drums.

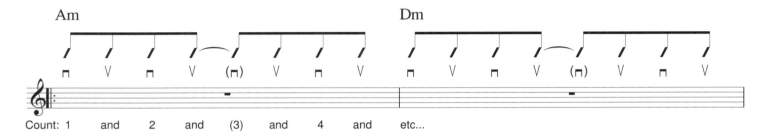

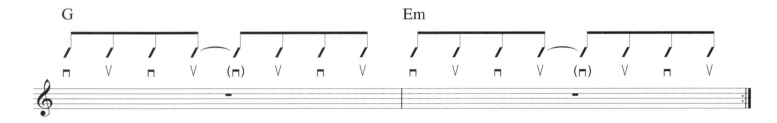

# Half Steps & Whole Steps

The distance in pitch between any two musical notes is called an interval. An interval is how much higher or lower one note sounds from another, or the space in between the notes. The smallest interval on the guitar is from a fretted note to the fret next to it on the same string.
This distance is called a half step. Twice the distance, or the distance of two frets, is called a whole step.

The musical alphabet uses the letters A through G. The distance from one letter or note to the next is usually a whole step (two frets), with two exceptions: there is only a half step between the notes B and C and between the notes E and F.

After counting up from A to G, we get to a higher sounding A and can continue to count up higher through the alphabet again from there. The distance from that first A to the next A (higher or lower) is called an octave.

# Power Chords

Power chords are simple two note chords that are used extensively in rock and metal. Power chords sound their fullest and heaviest when played with distortion. Below are two power chords shown at the 1st fret; both are played using just the first and third fingers.

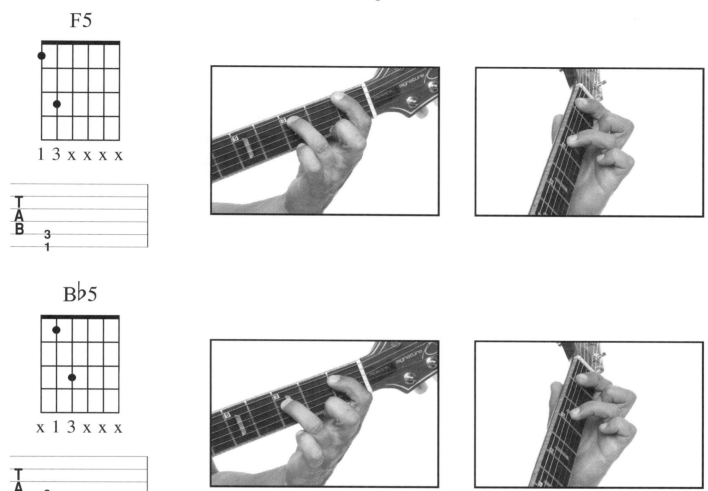

The two notes that make up power chords (also referred to as five chords) are called the root note and the fifth. The root note of the F5 power chord is F, the note that gives the chord its name. The other note is a C, which is the fifth note up the musical alphabet from the root note (F-G-A-B-C). These power chords are actually abbreviated versions of regular major and minor chords. Major and minor chords are made up of root notes, thirds and fifths. The third is the note which determines whether a chord is major or minor. Since power chords contain no thirds, they are neither major nor minor. Because of this, power chords can be an ideal choice for many different keys and styles.

Power chords are moveable chords; if you move the same fingering to another fret, the name of the chord changes. This is called transposing the chord. Notice that the lowest note of each power chord is the root note. Using the musical alphabet and the chromatic scale, you can transpose the power chords to any chord in the scale. For example, if you take the F5 chord and move it one whole step higher to the 3rd fret, it will become a G5 power chord. The chart below shows the notes along the 5th and 6th strings up to the 12th fret. You can use this chart to transpose the F5 and Bb5 power chords to any other fret.

| 6th string notes (F5 chord) | E | F | F♯ | G | G♯ | A | A♯ | B | C | C♯ | D | D♯ | E |
|---|---|---|---|---|---|---|---|---|---|---|---|---|---|
| fret number | Open | 1 | 2 | 3 | 4 | 5 | 6 | 7 | 8 | 9 | 10 | 11 | 12 |
| 5th string notes (B♭5 chord) | A | B♭ | B | C | C♯ | D | D♯ | E | F | F♯ | G | G♯ | A |

# Power Chord Progression

Here's a popular progression using all power chords. Use only your first and third fingers to fret each chord and practice moving smoothly from chord to chord. This exercise has been written in eighth notes, but you can experiment with the rhythm and strumming and come up with your own variations. Play along with the backing track and try it in different ways. Instead of eighth notes, try playing sixteenth notes, quarter notes or half notes. You can use alternate strumming, or try using all down strums to create a chunkier, metal sound. As you progress, you'll notice that the way you attack or strum the strings will make a big difference in the overall sound.

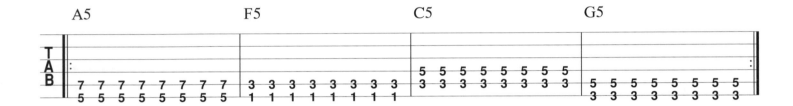

# The Chromatic Scale

Counting up or down the musical alphabet in half steps (or frets) is called a chromatic scale. The regular letters of the alphabet are called natural notes. Where there is a whole step between two natural notes, the note that falls in between them is a sharp (#) or flat (b) note. The # next to a note makes the note a half step higher. The b lowers the note a half step. For example, the note in between A and B can be called either an A# or a Bb since it's actually the same note with two different names. Whether you call a note sharp or flat depends on what key you're playing in or what the context is. The half steps that occur between B and C and between E and F (where there aren't other notes between them) are referred to as natural half steps. If you memorize where these two natural half steps occur you can use that knowledge to find any note on the guitar. Just start with any open string and count up in half steps.

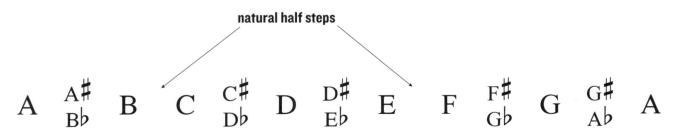

# Ascending Chromatic Scale

The following is an exercise that goes up through the chromatic scale in the 1st position of the guitar. Notice that when playing up the scale there are only twelve different notes until you reach an octave and start over with the same letters. These are the twelve notes that make up all music. The name of each note is written above the tab staff.

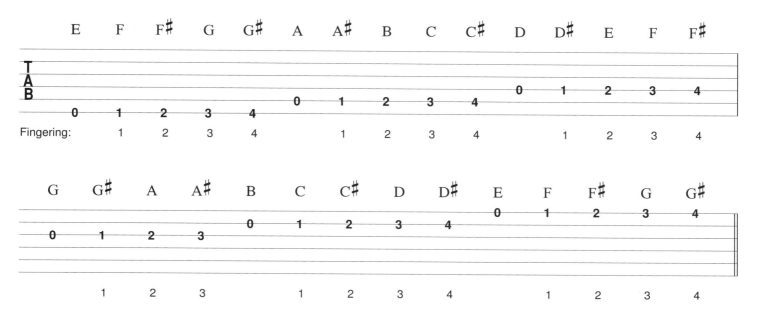

# Descending Chromatic Scale

Here's the first position chromatic scale in reverse, descending from highest to lowest note using all flats. Practice both the ascending and descending chromatic scales using the metronome to build up speed and coordination.

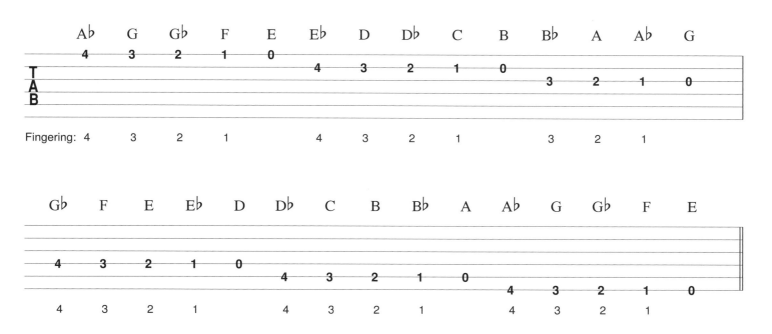

# Scale Diagrams

Scale diagrams are used to visually show you a scale pattern on the neck of a guitar. In this book you will see two different styles of scale diagrams that are very common.

## Diagram Type 1

The six lines that go from left to right represent each of the six strings. Like with tablature, the top line is the thinnest (highest pitched) string and the bottom line is the thickest (lowest pitched) string. The lines running from top to bottom are the frets. The numbered dots placed directly on a string show you the specific fret to play each note, and the number inside indicates which left hand finger to fret the note with (1 = index, 2 = middle, 3 = ring, 4 = pinky). The numbers underneath the diagram indicate where on the neck the scale is located, in this diagram the scale begins at the 5th fret:

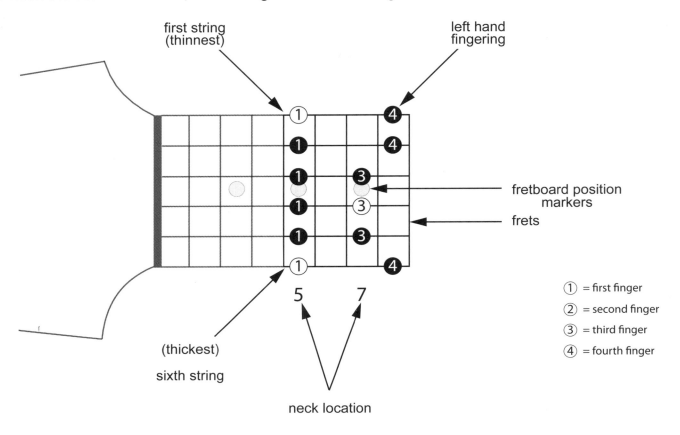

① = first finger

② = second finger

③ = third finger

④ = fourth finger

## Diagram Type 2

**C major scale**
**1st position**

Here is the second scale diagram style that will be used in this book which is similar to the chord diagrams you've seen in the previous lessons. This diagram is for the 1st position C major scale at the bottom of the next page. The stacked numbers below indicate the fingering for the notes on each string.

8fr

```
2  1  1  1  2  1
4  2  3  3  4  2
   4  4  4
```

# Constructing the Major Scale

Now that you have a firm understanding of the Chromatic scale, it is time to construct the major scale. As mentioned in the last chapter, the Chromatic scale is the basis of our musical keys. Much of Western Music is based upon the major scale. Have you ever heard: do re me fa so la ti do? If so, then you are already familiar with the major scale.

The major scale is constructed using five Whole-Steps and two Half-Steps. A Whole Step is the distance of two frets and a Half-Step is the distance of one fret on your guitar. The Half Steps connect the 3rd and 4th degrees and also the 7th and 8th degrees of the scale. The formula we use to create the major scale is: Whole Step – Whole Step – Half-Step – Whole Step – Whole Step – Whole Step – Half Step, many times they are depicted with single capitol letters as follows W – W – H – W – W – W – H. Applying this formula on any note of the chromatic scale will guide you to create a major scale. The starting note is also referred to as the "Root Note" and this is the name of the scale or key. Let's look at a C chromatic scale and apply the Whole Step Half-Step formula to create a C major scale.

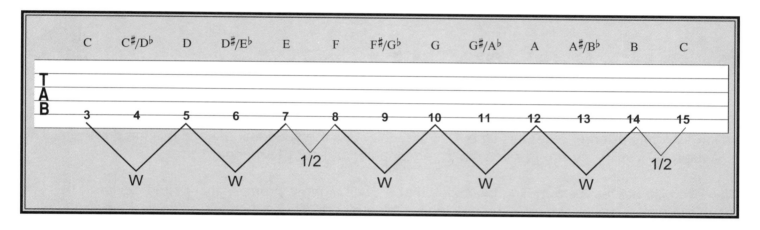

Playing the scale across one string isn't the most versatile way to play the guitar. So we take the notes C – D – E – F – G – A – B & C and apply them to a position. A position is the technical term for a four fret span on the neck of your guitar.

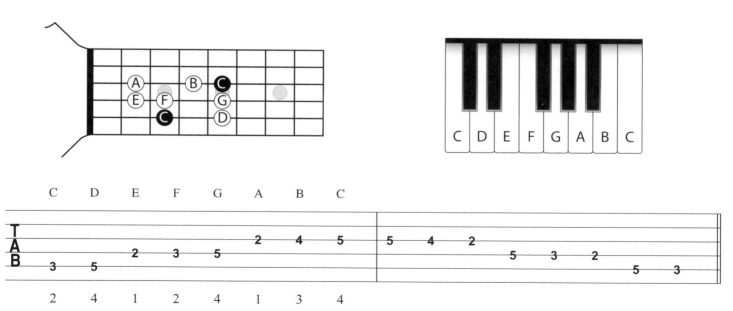

31

# Intervals of the Major Scale

The sequence of whole steps and half steps is what gives a scale or key its tonality. There is a specific sequence of intervals for a major scale and this formula is the same no matter what key the major scale is in. In the chart below, you can see that within the major scale the half steps fall between the 3rd and 4th steps and between the 7th and the octave. All of the other intervals are whole steps. This will be true for any major scale. All together in order, the sequence of intervals (steps) for a major scale are whole - whole - half - whole - whole - whole - half. Scale steps are numbered using roman numerals. The tonic, subdominant, and dominant (I - IV - V) are capitalized because they represent the major chords in the key.

| whole step | whole step | half step | whole step | whole step | whole step | half step | |
|---|---|---|---|---|---|---|---|
| C | D | E | F | G | A | B | C |
| I | ii | iii | IV | V | vi | vii | I |

# Acoustic Rock Chord Progression

The following chord progression is in the key of D major. Notice that it uses the I - IV – V chords of the key in a slightly different order this time. D is the tonic, G is the subdominant and A is the dominant. This is actually a I - V - IV - V progression that's very popular and easy to recognize.

This exercise utilizes a strumming technique that we call a ghost strum. A ghost strum occurs when you move the pick over the strings without actually striking them. This allows you to keep your arm moving in a constant down-up-down motion, keeping your playing fluid and in time. The strumming symbols in parentheses indicate where ghost strums occur.

The rhythm used is an example of syncopation. You're playing a syncopated rhythm if there's one or more strums off the beat, or on the upbeat instead of the downbeat. The strum on beat 2 1/2 is tied to beat 3, so you don't strum directly on beat 3.

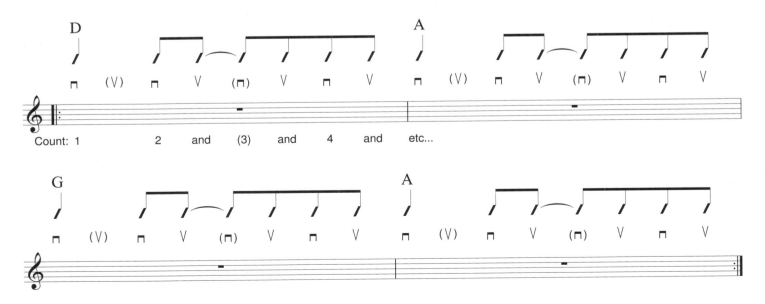

If you're having trouble changing from chord to chord smoothly, isolate the change and just practice going back and forth between those two chords. With practice, you'll build finger memory and your fingers will instinctively know where to go. Play this rhythm along with the backing track and get the changes, the feel and the strumming motion down.

# Making Melodies

Now it's time to start creating some melodies and leads. Let's take the C major scale you just learned and move the entire pattern up one whole step (two frets), so that your second finger is at the 10th fret on the note D. If you play the exact same pattern from there, you will have a D major scale. This is called transposing the scale.

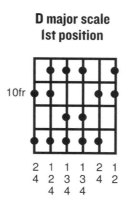

**D major scale**
**Ist position**

10fr

```
2 1 1 1 2 1
4 2 3 3 4 2
  4 4 4
```

## The D Major Scale

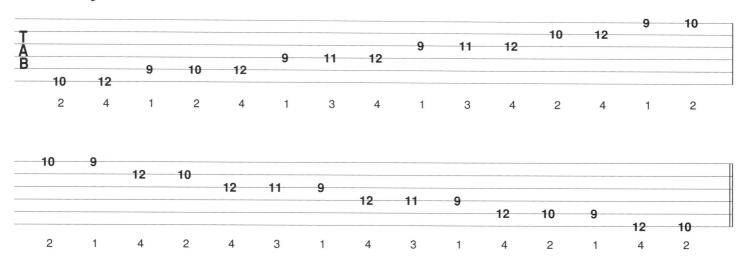

Remember that the key of C major is the only key made up of all natural notes. When the major scale is transposed to a different key, accidentals (sharps or flats) need to be added to some of the notes. This is to make sure that all of the whole steps and half steps are between the proper steps of the scale. For example, if you start on D (the root note), the second note of the scale is E and the third note is an F. In the major scale formula, there has to be a whole step between the 2nd and 3rd steps. Since there is a natural half step between E and F, you need to add a sharp to the F to make it a whole step up from E. The C also needs to be sharped to have a whole step between the 6th and 7th steps. The key of D major contains two sharps.

| | whole step | | whole step | | half step | | whole step | | whole step | | whole step | | half step | |
|---|---|---|---|---|---|---|---|---|---|---|---|---|---|---|---|
| D | | E | | F♯ | | G | | A | | B | | C♯ | | D |
| I | | ii | | iii | | IV | | V | | vi | | vii | | I |

# Improvising

You can play the D major scale along with the Acoustic Rock Chord Progression from the previous lesson and start to learn how to play solos. Play along with the backing track and experiment with the notes to create your own little melodies. You can start by playing up or down the scale, then mix it up a little. Play small parts of the scale in sections, hold some notes out longer than others and try to ascend or descend a few notes at a time. Avoid just playing the entire two octave scale all at once; you only need to use a few notes to come up with the most memorable and tasteful melodies. Keep it simple, follow your ear and listen for which notes sound good to you and in what order. Use your instinct and let your creative side come out.

Here is an example of some melodies you can play. For your reference, the chord names are located above the staff. On the video that follows along with this book, note that these melodies were improvised during the lesson as an example. This solo has been tabbed out here to get you started and show you how it's done. The point of this lesson is for you to understand how to improvise, so don't get caught up in trying to learn this example note for note. Instead, take a quick look through these riffs and then spend more time creating your own.

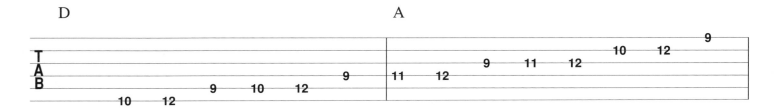

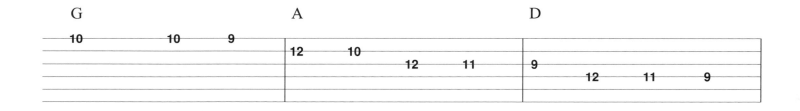

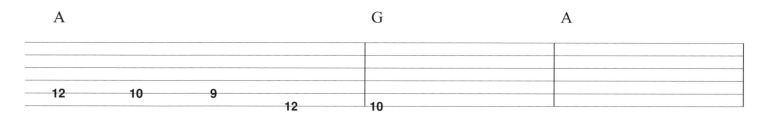

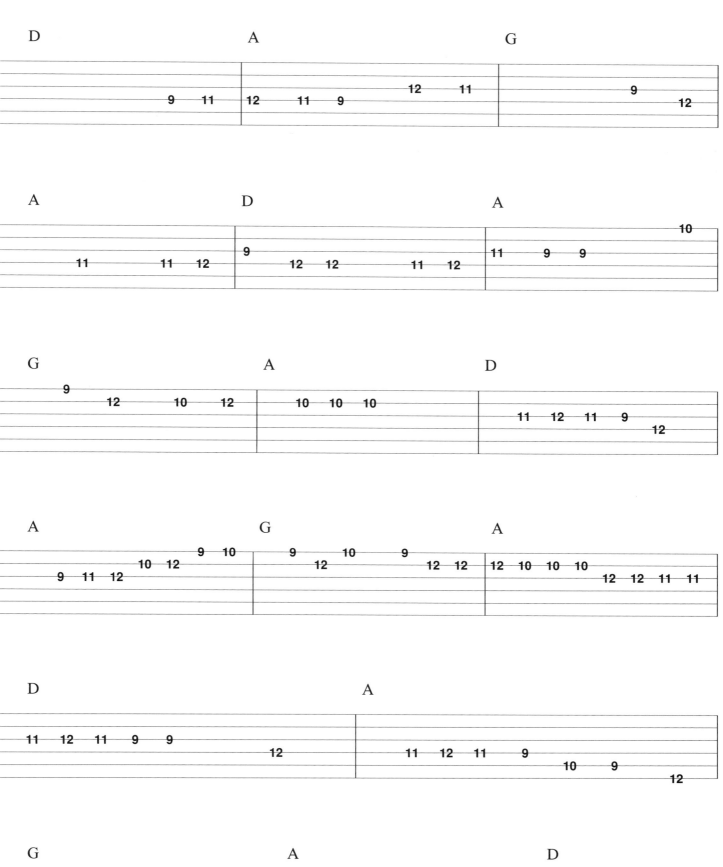

# Single Note Blues Rhythm

Here's a shuffle rhythm guitar progression consisting of all single notes. This pattern is a good example of a riff. The riff is outlined in the first measure. As the progression follows a 12-bar blues, the riff is transposed to each new chord. This example is also based around a I - IV – V chord change in the key of D (D - G - A). Once you have this progression down, try to create some of your own single note riff rhythms.

D

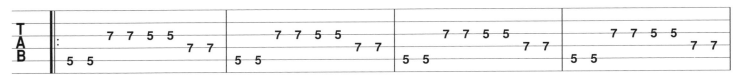

Fingering: 1  1  3  3  1  1  3  3    1  1  3  3  1  1  3  3    1  1  3  3  1  1  3  3    1  1  3  3  1  1  3  3

G                                                            D

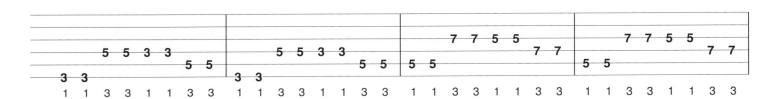

1  1  3  3  1  1  3  3    1  1  3  3  1  1  3  3    1  1  3  3  1  1  3  3    1  1  3  3  1  1  3  3

A                                                            D

1  1  3  3  1  1  3  3    1  1  3  3  1  1  3  3    1  1  3  3  1  1  3  3    1  1  3  3  1  1  3  3

# Alternate Picking Chords

Let's start this section with an alternate picking exercise to help coordinate your right hand. Instead of strumming the chords, you might pick the notes of a chord out individually and let them ring out together.

Fret an open D chord and hold the chord shape with your left hand while picking out the individual notes in the order notated on the tab staff. This picking pattern (indicated by which number string you pick) is 4 - 1 - 3 - 1 - 2 - 1. Recite the string number while you pick each one to help memorize the order. Use a down-up-down-up alternate picking pattern. Notice that the 1st string is always up picked, while the other strings are all down picked. Try to hold one of your right hand fingers on the body of the guitar to help give you added support and control. Practice playing in a steady, even rhythm, in time with a metronome.

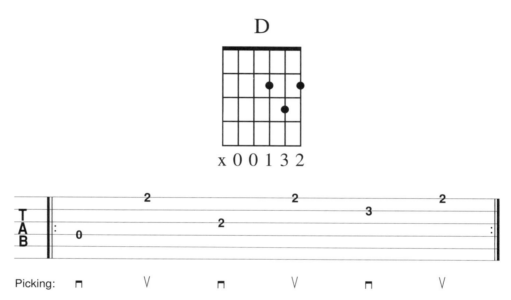

You can use this pattern for the other chords too. Here's the same pattern with a C chord. Once you get the alternate picking motion down, get creative and come up with your own patterns.

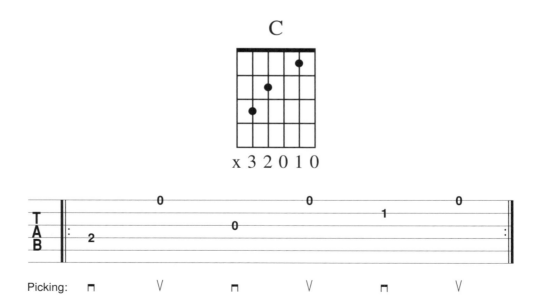

# Drop D Tuning

Drop D tuning refers to lowering the pitch of the 6th string from E to D. This gives the guitar a heavier, meaner sound. To tune your guitar to Drop D tuning, strike the open 4th string (D) and the open 6th string together. Gradually lower the 6th string from E to D until the 4th and 6th strings sound "in tune" with each other. These two strings are now both tuned to D an octave apart from each other. You can check your tuning using the online tuner at www.rockhousemethod.com to make sure you've got it.

Rhythms are extremely easy to play in Drop D because the 6th string power chords are now played with just one finger. Simply barre one finger across the lowest three strings at any fret. You can also play a D5 chord just by strumming the lowest three open strings. Below are three chord diagrams to give you some ideas on how to use Drop D tuning to play chords.

### D5
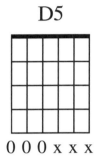

0 0 0 x x x

### F5

1 1 1 x x x

### G5
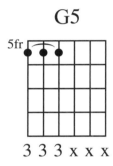

3 3 3 x x x

# Drop D Metal Rhythm

The following rhythm is a popular heavy metal style riff in Drop D tuning. Play along with the heavy metal bass and drum backing track and get comfortable with the syncopated chord change. Try muting the strings by lightly touching the side of your picking hand against the strings right after the strings come off the bridge. If you move too far away from the bridge, you'll end up deadening the strings instead of getting the proper muted sound. This technique is called palm muting and is common in rock and metal. After you've got this example down, experiment and create your own rhythms and riffs in Drop D tuning.

| D5 | F5 | G5 | D5 | F5 | G5 |
|---|---|---|---|---|---|

```
T
A ||: 0   0   0   3   3   3   5   5 | 0   0   0   3   3   3   5   5
B    0   0   0   3   3   3   5   5 | 0   0   0   3   3   3   5   5
     0   0   0   3   3   3   5   5 | 0   0   0   3   3   3   5   5
```

| D5 | F5 | G5 | D5 | | | | | | |
|---|---|---|---|---|---|---|---|---|---|

```
  0   0   0   3   3   3   5   5 | 0   0   0   0   0   0   0   0 :||
  0   0   0   3   3   3   5   5 | 0   0   0   0   0   0   0   0
  0   0   0   3   3   3   5   5 | 0   0   0   0   0   0   0   0
```

# Essential Barre Chords

## Major and Minor Barre Chords

Two very important chords are the F and Bb barre chords. These are full barre chords containing no open strings, so they are moveable chords. You can transpose them to any fret.

Full barre chords are especially difficult to play. For the F barre chord, you need to barre your first finger across all six strings, then add the other three notes as well. Pick out each note individually to make sure it sounds clean and you've got it down. After mastering these chords, you'll be able to play in any key and position on the guitar.

1 3 4 2 1 1

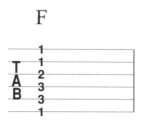

Notice that the lowest note of the chord is the root note. Using the musical alphabet and the chromatic scale from Chapter 3, you can move full barre chords up the neck and change them to any chord in the scale. Use the following chart to find any chord along the 6th string by moving the F chord.

| 6th string notes (F chord) | E | F | F♯ | G | G♯ | A | A♯ | B | C | C♯ | D | D♯ | E |
|---|---|---|---|---|---|---|---|---|---|---|---|---|---|
| fret number | Open | 1 | 2 | 3 | 4 | 5 | 6 | 7 | 8 | 9 | 10 | 11 | 12 |
| 5th string notes (Bb chord) | A | B♭ | B | C | C♯ | D | D♯ | E | F | F♯ | G | G♯ | A |

For the Bb chord, you need to barre across three strings with your third finger. The Fm and Bbm chords are only slightly different. All of these chords are also moveable using the chart.

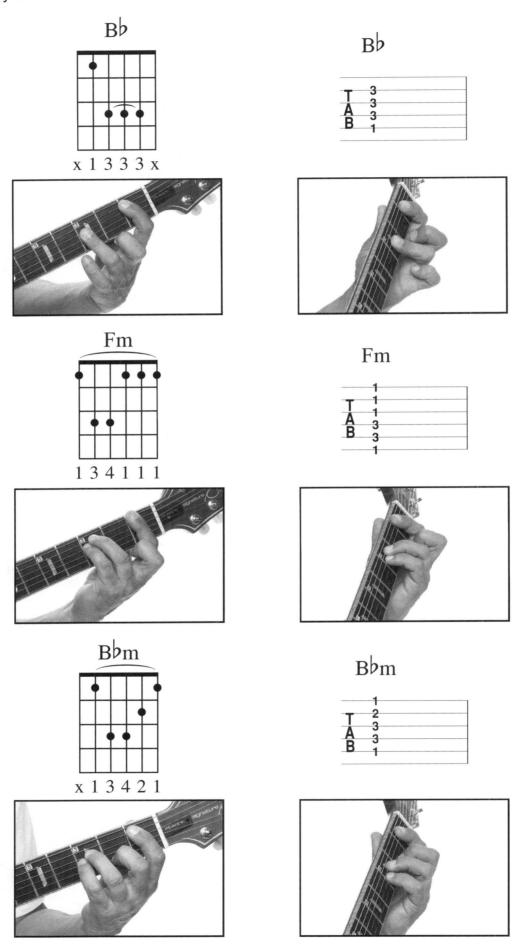

# Major Seventh and Minor Seventh Chords

Now let's move on to the major 7th (maj7) and minor 7th (m7) barre chords, which are also all moveable. The 7th chords are extensions of the original major and minor chords - they add a new note to the chord which gives it more flavor and a jazzier sound.

For the Gmaj7 chord, you need to mute or deaden the 5th string with your fretting hand. If you tilt your first finger down slightly, it will lightly touch the 5th string and mute it. The Cmaj7 chord doesn't use a barre, which makes it slightly easier to play. In both chords, the 1st string is not strummed.

Gmaj7

1 x 3 4 2 x

Gmaj7

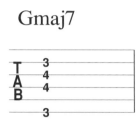

```
T----------3-------
A----------4-------
B----------4-------
----------3-------
```

Cmaj7

3fr

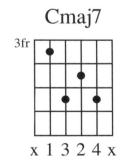

x 1 3 2 4 x

Cmaj7

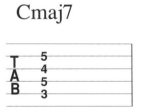

```
T----------5-------
A----------4-------
B----------5-------
----------3-------
```

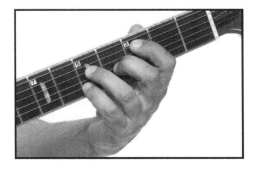

From the minor barre chords you've just learned, all you need to do is lift your pinky off either chord and you'll have the minor 7th chords: Fm7 and Bbm7.

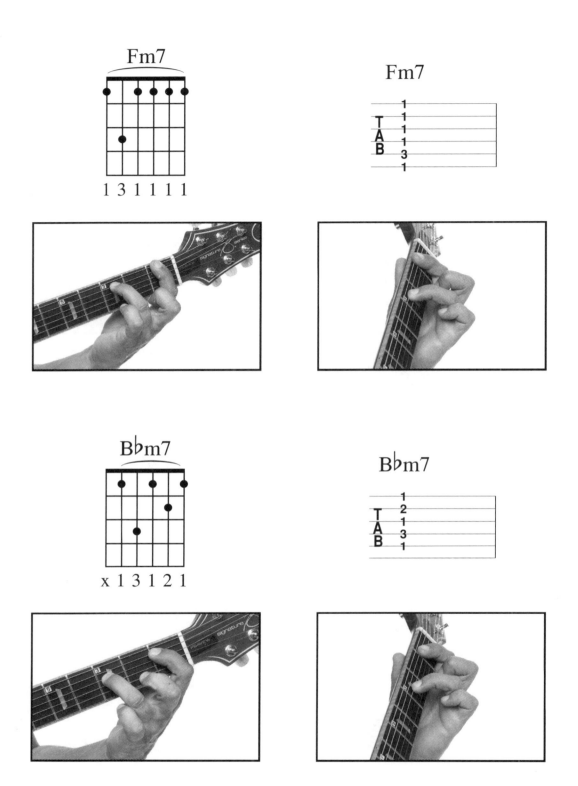

Memorize and practice all of the moveable barre chords. Make sure you have them down perfectly and can play them cleanly because we'll be using them in the upcoming sections. All of these chords are essential for playing rock and blues.

# Arpeggio Chord Progression

An arpeggio is defined as the notes of a chord played separately. In this exercise, fret a C major chord and pick the notes separately in their order on the tab staff. Next, change to the Em chord. Here you can use a slightly different fingering for the Em that will make it easier to change chords. Just leave your second finger in the same place for both chords. The left hand fingering is notated under the tab staff. Pick the notes in the sequence indicated while holding down the chord fingering, allowing the notes to ring out.

This is a common pattern used in ballads and slow tempo songs. Listen to the backing track and play along. Notice the timing is different than the regular 4/4 (four beats per measure) we've been playing up until now. This rhythm only contains three quarter notes per measure, counted: "One, two, three, one, two, three." A waltz is a good example of 3/4 time. The picking pattern here is also different. Instead of alternate picking, down pick the lower strings in a row, then up pick the higher strings.

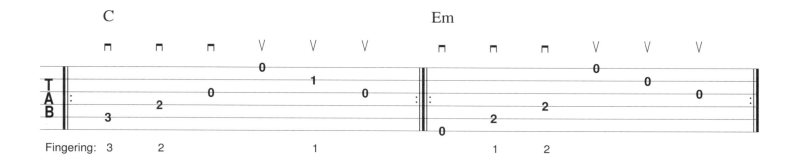

# Changing the Feel of a Song

By altering the strumming or picking pattern of a chord progression, you can dramatically change the style. In this section, we'll show you how to take a simple chord change and use it to play many different genres of music, all against the same bass and drum backing track. This demonstrates the power of the guitar and its ability to dictate the feel of the song.

A Cadd9 chord (or a Csus2 chord) is a slight variation of the regular C chord. Notice how similar the fingering is to the G chord and how easy it is to switch back and forth between them. Just leave your third and fourth fingers stationary and move your first and second fingers up or down one string.

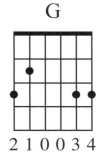

G

2 1 0 0 3 4

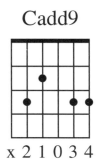

Cadd9

x 2 1 0 3 4

## Rock

This is a standard rock rhythm you've already played using the new progression.

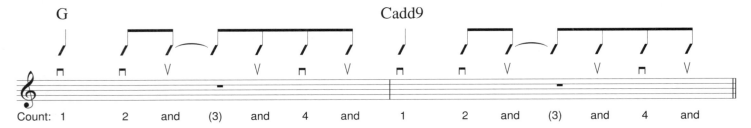

## Reggae

Reggae uses all upstrokes. Following each up strum of the pick, mute the strings with your picking hand in time and on the downbeat to give it that reggae feel.

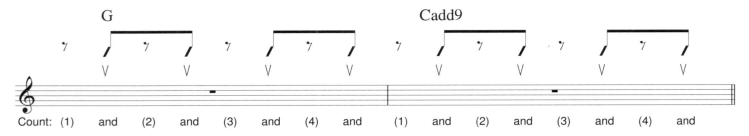

## Ballad

Here's another rock ballad pattern. Use the same picking technique from the previous lesson, Down picking the first half of the measure and up picking the second half.

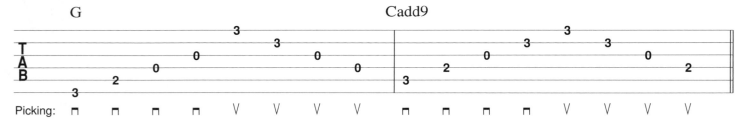

## Country

Country guitar rhythms alternate between picking and strumming. Pick the lower notes on the downbeats, and follow the picked notes with regular strums on the upbeats.

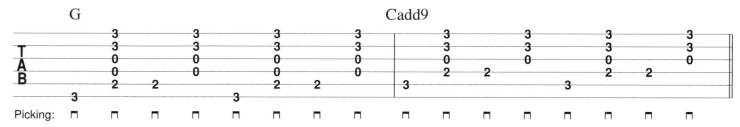

# Fingerpicking

When applying the fingerpicking technique to the guitar, use only your fingers to play the notes and chords; no pick is used. Pluck downward with your thumb and upward with your fingers. Thumb and fingers are labeled as p (thumb), i (index), m (middle), a (ring finger). These are international finger picking symbols.

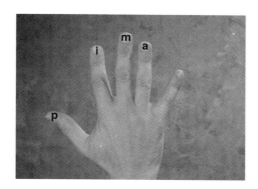

In the following exercise, fret and hold the chord (D, Cadd9 or G) and pick out the notes in their order on the tab staff. Use the letters underneath to show you which right hand fingers to use. There are also many hybrid ways to fingerpick; for example using your pick, but also incorporating some of your fingers to pluck the strings. Once you have this technique down, have fun experimenting with it.

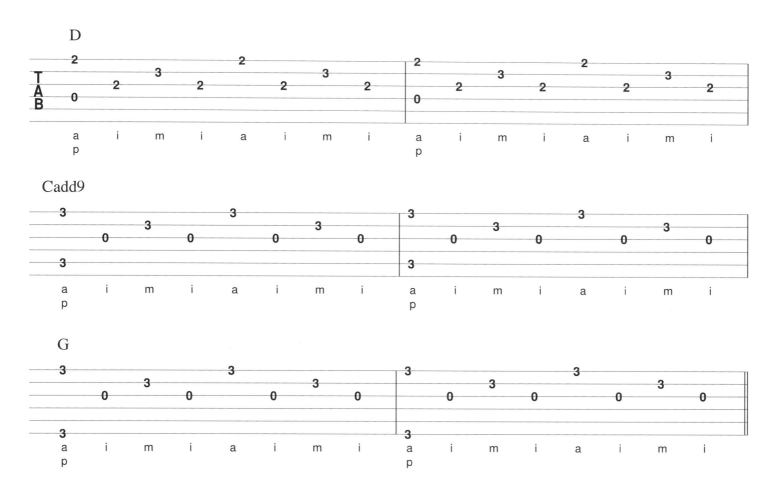

# Major Seventh Chord Progression

Now let's take the major seventh chords from the last chapter and play them at the 5th fret: Amaj7 and Dmaj7. The rhythm for this progression is syncopated, so use the same basic ghost strumming technique you learned earlier to help keep a smooth, pendulum motion with your right arm. Practice this progression along with the backing track that's available at the Lesson Support Site.

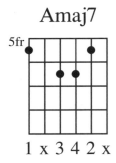

Amaj7
5fr
1 x 3 4 2 x

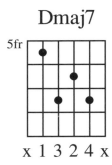

Dmaj7
5fr
x 1 3 2 4 x

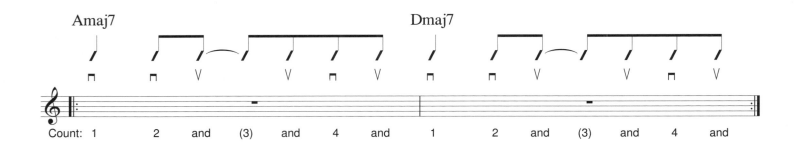

# Using the Metronome to Practice

As you progress as a guitarist you can use the metronome in your daily practice to help keep a steady rhythm and gauge your progress. Here are a few metronome practice tips that will help you use this tool effectively.

1. When starting to learn a new song set the metronome at a slow tempo where you can play the entire piece through without making mistakes.

2. Gradually build your speed by increasing the BPM (beats per minute) on the metronome a few numbers each day.

3. As you play with the metronome try not to focus on it too much. Sense the feel of the click and concentrate on the song you are playing.

# The Minor Pentatonic Scale

Minor pentatonic scales are the most commonly used scales for playing rock and blues solos. The pentatonic is a five note scale, or an abbreviated version of the full natural minor scale. The word "pentatonic" comes from the greek words, "penta" (five) and "tonic" (the keynote).

Memorize and practice this scale; it's the one you'll use most often for playing melodies and leads. There are five different positions of this scale, each beginning on a different note of the scale. All five positions are shown here in tab. To the right of each tab staff is a scale diagram. These are similar to the chord diagrams we've previously used. A scale diagram shows you all the notes in the scale within a certain position on the neck. The stacked numbers below the diagram indicate the fingering for the notes on each string.

## 1st Position A Minor Pentatonic Scale

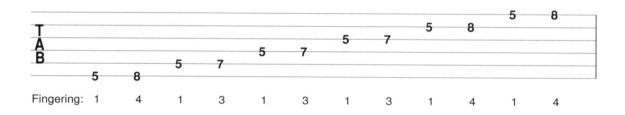

## 2nd Position A Minor Pentatonic Scale

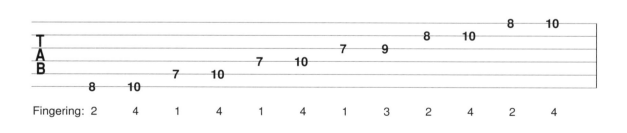

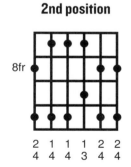

## 3rd Position A Minor Pentatonic Scale

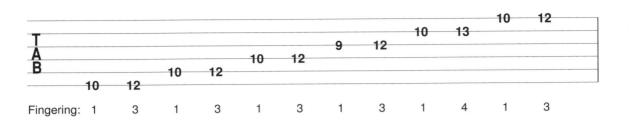
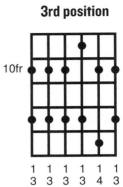

**3rd position**

Fingering:  1   3   1   3   1   3   1   3   1   4   1   3

## 4th Position A Minor Pentatonic Scale

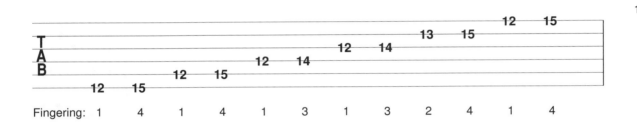
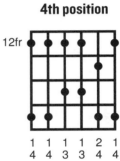

**4th position**

Fingering:  1   4   1   4   1   3   1   3   2   4   1   4

## 5th Position A Minor Pentatonic Scale

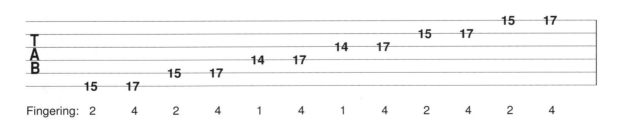
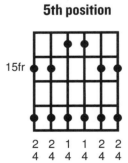

**5th position**

Fingering:  2   4   2   4   1   4   1   4   2   4   2   4

## The Minor Pentatonic Scale Fretboard Diagram

Once you have all five positions of the minor pentatonic scales mastered, you'll be able to play solos in any position on the neck. Remember that there are only five different name notes in the scale, and the different positions are just groupings of these same notes in different octaves and different places on the neck. The 4th and 5th positions from the previous page can be transposed one octave lower (shown below in the fretboard diagram). Notice how each position overlaps the next; the left side of one position is the right side of the next one and so on. Think of these scale positions as building blocks (like Legos). When soloing, you can move from position to position and play across the entire fretboard.

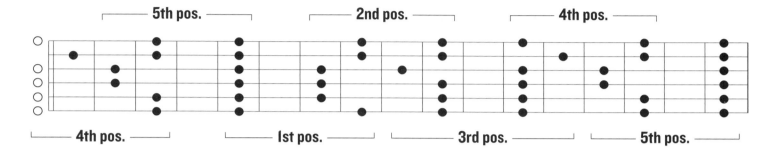

# Bending

Now let's learn some lead guitar techniques that will add expression to your playing. Bends are a very soulful way of creating emotion with the guitar, using flesh against steel to alter and control pitches. All guitarists have their own unique, signature way of bending notes.

The row of tab staffs below shows bends using the third, fourth or first fingers. The "B" above the staff indicates a bend, and the arrow with a "1" above it means to bend the note one whole step in pitch.

First try the third finger bend. While fretting the note with your third finger, keep your first two fingers down on the string behind it and push upward using all three fingers. This will give you added coordination and control.

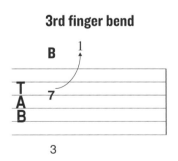

Use the same technique for the fourth finger bend, using all four fingers to bend the string upward. The first finger bend will probably be the hardest since you are only using one finger to bend the string. In some situations, you may even pull the string downward with your first finger to bend the note.

**4th finger bend**

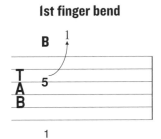

**Ist finger bend**

The following example shows what the bends might look like in context when playing a solo in the 1st position A minor pentatonic scale. Play through this exercise and start to get a feel for how to incorporate bends into your own riffs.

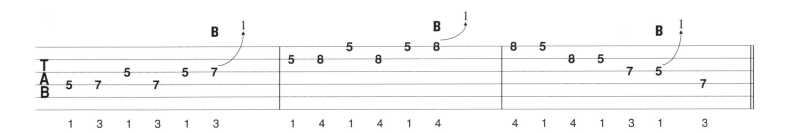

## Quick Quote!

"The Blues are the true facts of life expressed in words and song, inspiration, feeling, and understanding. "

- Willie Dixon

# Hammer Ons and Pull Offs

Hammer ons and pull offs are two more widely used lead techniques. On the staffs below, you'll see a slur connecting one tab number to the next. This indicates that only the first tab number is picked; the second note is not struck. The "H" above the slur indicates a hammer on, and the "P" indicates a pull off.

To play a hammer on, pick the first note and then push down the next note using just your left hand finger (without picking it). Play through the series of hammer ons in the first measure below to see how you can use these with the minor pentatonic scale.

Pull offs are the opposite of hammer ons. Pick the first note and pull or snap your finger off the string to the get the second note. Your first finger should already be in place, fretting the second note in advance.

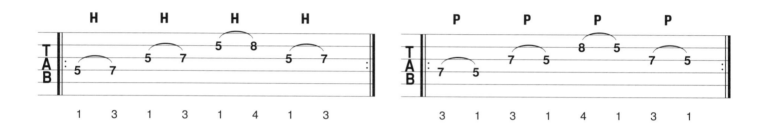

The following exercise contains hammer ons and pull offs in combination. The slurs encompass three notes; so only pick the first one. Hammer on for the second note, then pull off to the third note. At the very end of the second measure, you'll see a squiggly line above the last note. This line indicates a technique known as vibrato. While sustaining the note, shake your finger slightly and "dig in" to the note to vibrate the pitch and give it more expression.

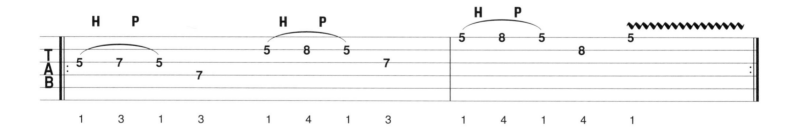

# Complete Rhythm & Lead

For the last section of this chapter we'll use a complete rock rhythm and show you how to solo over it. First learn the following barre chord rhythm and play it along with the backing track.

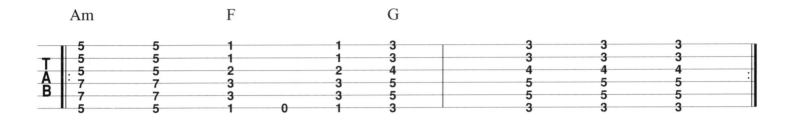

The following guitar solo incorporates all of the lead techniques and covers several positions of the minor pentatonic scale. After you've got this lead down, get creative and try improvising along with the backing track in every position of the A minor pentatonic using bends, hammer ons and pull offs. You should now have a solid foundation for playing your own rock and blues solos.

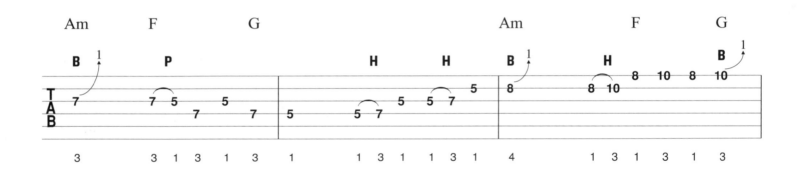

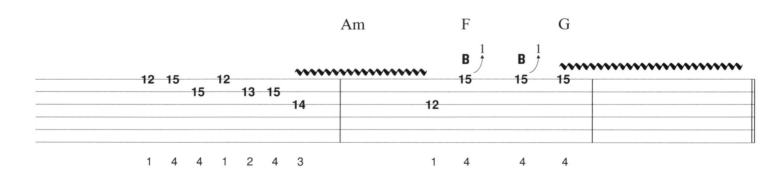

52

# Transposing the Minor Pentatonic Scale

You can solo over the single note blues rhythm by transposing the minor pentatonic scale to D. Each of the five positions can be moved to a different fret, allowing you to solo in any key anywhere on the fretboard. For instance, if you were to move all of the A minor pentatonic scale positions two frets (one whole step) higher, you would be playing in B.

The following chart shows the minor pentatonic scale in some popular keys, indicating where each position starts by fret. Choose a key from the left hand column and follow the chart across to see which fret each position starts on. Since an octave is only 12 frets, some positions can be played in two different places on the neck.

| key | 1st position | 2nd position | 3rd position | 4th position | 5th position |
|---|---|---|---|---|---|
| A | 5th & 17th frets | 8th fret | 10th fret | 12th fret & open | 3rd & 15th frets |
| C | 8th fret | 11th fret | 13th & 1st frets | 3rd & 15th frets | 6th & 18th frets |
| E | 12th fret & open | 3rd & 15th frets | 5th & 17th frets | 7th fret | 10th fret |
| G | 3rd & 15th frets | 6th & 18th frets | 8th fret | 10th fret | 13th & 1st frets |
| B | 7th & 19th frets | 10th fret | 12th fret | 14th & 2nd frets | 5th & 17th frets |
| D | 10th fret | 13th & 1st frets | 3rd & 15th frets | 5th & 17th frets | 8th fret |
| F | 1st & 13th frets | 4th & 16th frets | 6th & 18th frets | 8th fret | 11th fret |

# Lead Patterns

The following examples are standard lead pattern exercises, designed to help you build coordination and learn how to begin using the minor pentatonics for playing leads. Use alternate picking and the metronome to start out slowly and get the rhythm. Memorize the patterns and gradually speed up the tempo. Before you know it, you'll be playing blazing rock and blues guitar solos.

## Double Lead Pattern

Here is the 1st position A minor pentatonic scale played in groups of three notes, or triplets. Count "one - two - three, one - two - three" out loud while you play through this exercise to get the triplet feel in your head.

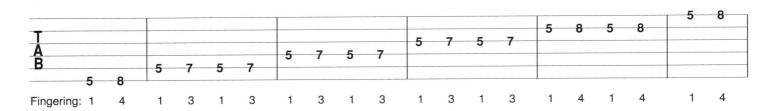

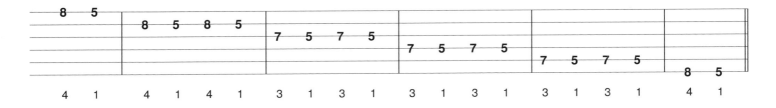

Now let's take the same double lead pattern and transpose it to the 2nd position. Once you've got these two memorized, transpose the pattern to the other positions of the pentatonic scale.

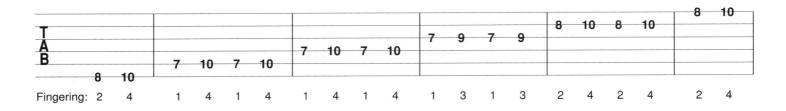

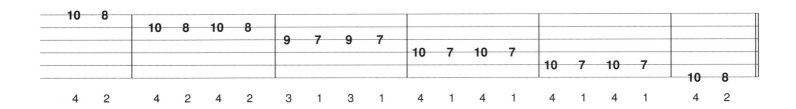

# Triplet Lead Pattern

Here is the 1st position A minor pentatonic scale played in groups of three notes, or triplets. Count "one - two - three, one - two - three" out loud while you play through this exercise to get the triplet feel in your head.

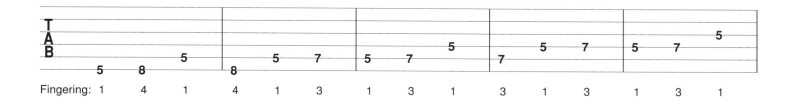

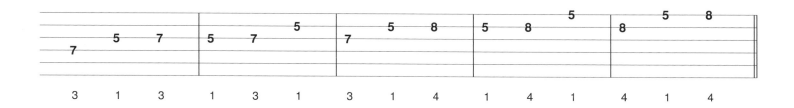

Now let's play the same pattern in reverse, back down the scale in triplets.

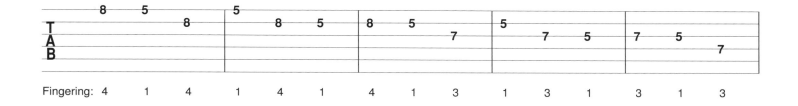

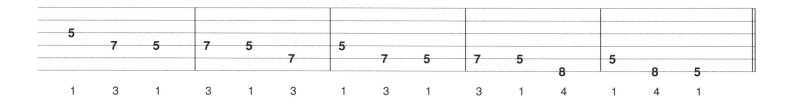

Practice every position of the A minor pentatonic scale using the triplet lead pattern and alternate picking. The 2nd position ascending and descending triplet patterns are shown below.

# Complete Blues Lead

Here's a solo that uses all of the previous lead techniques in various positions on the neck. In the 11th measure, there's an example of a bend and release: after bending the note, gradually release the bend to the note's original pitch.

Refer to the CD or download the backing track from www.rockhousemethod.com and practice playing along with the band. This is a I - IV - V progression in A that also uses a shuffle feel. The chord names above the tab staff are there for a reference to show you where the changes are.

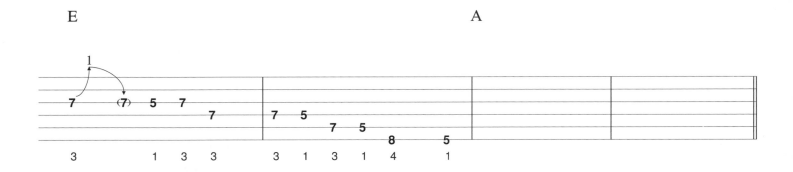

# Acoustic Rock Rhythm

Here's a popular acoustic rock rhythm using all barre chords. Play along to the backing track and get the quick strumming feel down. You can take all of the chords you've learned and play them in this or any other rhythm, then try writing some of your own songs.

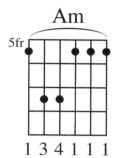

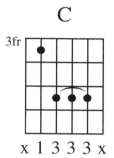
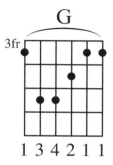

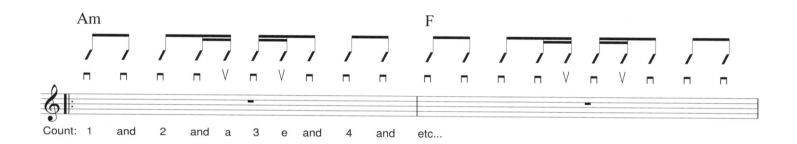

Count:  1   and   2   and   a   3   e   and   4   and   etc...

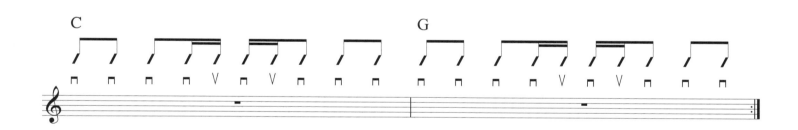

# Using the Capo

A capo (pronounced kay-po) is an accessory used to instantly transpose the entire guitar. There are different types of capos available ranging from clamp capos (shown below) to capos with an elastic material that wraps around the neck to keep it in place. A capo essentially barres across all six strings of the guitar, transposing all of the open strings up to the fret where the capo is placed. The capo can be used like a moveable nut; wherever the capo is placed becomes the new open position. All of the open chords can be played relative to the capo, which automatically transposes them to the new key. A capo is a very versatile and inexpensive accessory.

The photos below show a clamp capo being properly placed at the 2nd fret. Capos are popular at the 1st, 2nd, 3rd, 5th and 7th frets, but you can place a capo anywhere at all on the neck. A capo at the 12th fret transposes the guitar one octave higher and gives it a bright, mandolin tone. When there are multiple guitars playing at the same time, it's common to have one or more guitars capoed at different frets. This helps to create a fuller sound by having individual guitars playing the same progression transposed to different keys and different places on the neck.

Placing a clamp capo on the neck.

A capo properly placed at the 2nd fret.

Generally, capoed guitar parts are shown in tab relative to the placement of the capo. The music will be transposed to show the part as it would normally be shown in open position. The zeros in the tab are actually the fret that the capo is placed at. Try the following D major progression below, then place the capo at the 5th fret and play the same progression. The progression has now been transposed up to G major, and although you're still fingering D, G, and A chords, the actual sounding chords would be G, C and D. By placing the capo at the 7th fret, the progression will be transposed up to A major and the actual sounding chords will be A, D and E.

```
      D                           G                       A
    ⊓    ⊓   V   V   ⊓  V   etc.
     2   2  2    2  2  2    3   3  3   3  3  3
  T  3   3  3    3  3  3    3   3  3   3  3  3   2   2  2   2  2  2    2   2  2   2  2  2
  A‖: 2  2  2    2  2  2    0   0  0   0  0  0   2   2  2   2  2  2    2   2  2   2  2  2 :‖
  B‖  0  0  0    0  0  0    0   0  0   0  0  0   2   2  2   2  2  2    2   2  2   2  2  2
     0   0  0    0  0  0    2   2  2   2  2  2   0   0  0   0  0  0    0   0  0   0  0  0
                           3   3  3   3  3  3
```

# Blues Riffs That Will Make Yo Mama Scream

Here's a collection of little riffs that will help you start building your own bag of tricks. These riffs use various positions of the A minor pentatonic scales, and incorporate all of the techniques we've covered so far. You can play all of these riffs at different speeds, with or without a shuffle feel, starting on any beat you choose. Any one of these is a good choice when soloing and improvising. Try coming up with some of your own variations.

### Riff #1

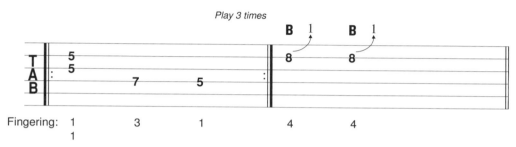

### Riff #2

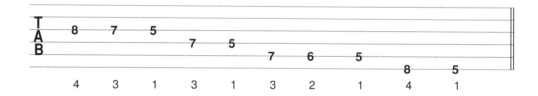

### Riff #3

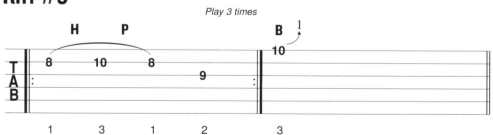

## Riff #4

*Play 4 times*

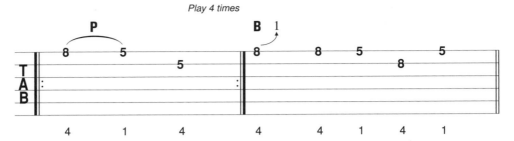

## Riff #5

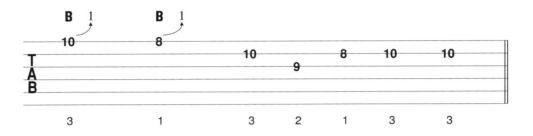

## Quick Tip!

### DEVELOP GOOD PRACTICE HABITS

*Knowing how to practice efficiently will accelerate your progress. Set aside a certain amount of time for practicing and have a routine that reviews all of the techniques you know. Create your own exercises that target weaknesses in your playing. It's important to experiment and get creative as well; try things fast or slow, light or hard, soft or loud.*

# Shuffle Blues Rhythm

This progression incorporates chords and single notes to make up the rhythm. This standard blues rhythm is in A and uses a I - IV - V progression. Practice along with the backing track to get the timing and the shuffle feel.

A

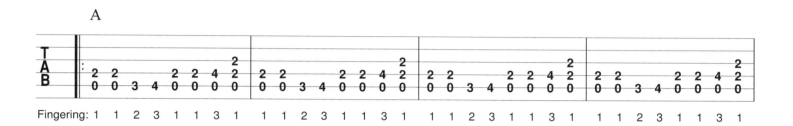

Fingering: 1 1 2 3 1 1 3 1   1 1 2 3 1 1 3 1   1 1 2 3 1 1 3 1   1 1 2 3 1 1 3 1

D                                                          A

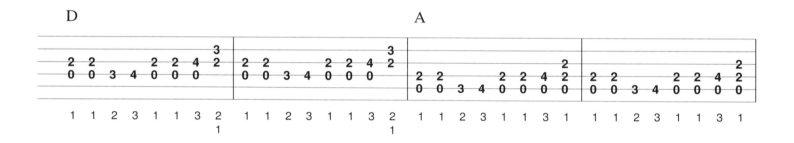

1 1 2 3 1 1 3 2   1 1 2 3 1 1 3 2   1 1 2 3 1 1 3 1   1 1 2 3 1 1 3 1
              1                 1

E                                                          A

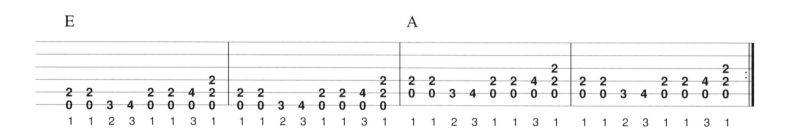

1 1 2 3 1 1 3 1   1 1 2 3 1 1 3 1   1 1 2 3 1 1 3 1   1 1 2 3 1 1 3 1

# The BB Box

The BB Box is a section of the minor pentatonic scale that overlaps the 1st and 2nd positions. The name refers to the great B.B. King because he bases a lot of his soloing around this part of the scale. The following fretboard diagram indicates which notes are in the BB Box (in the key of Am) using solid black dots. The open circles show the minor pentatonic scale notes in the surrounding positions. Refer to the tab staff below the diagram for the proper fingering.

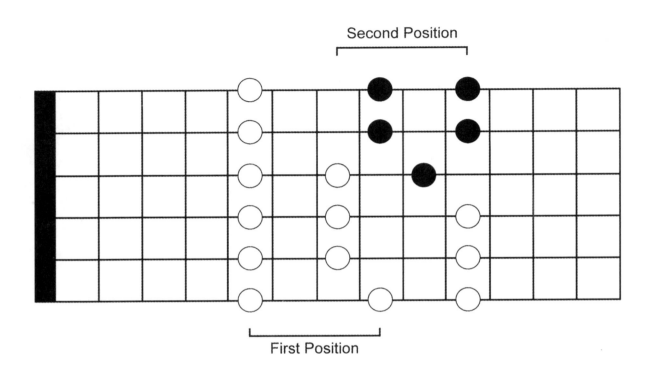

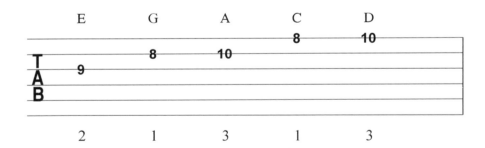

Above each tab number is its note name. Notice that A (the root note) is in between the other notes of the scale. The B.B. Box takes the five notes of the minor pentatonic scale and puts the root note in the middle. This position allows you to play around the root note, playing a few notes up or a few notes down from it. This is also the way many blues singers arrange their vocal melodies. The B.B. Box is great for soloing off the vocal melody or for trading riffs back and forth with the singer.

# Open E Tuning

Open tuning refers to the act of tuning all of the strings on the guitar to the notes of a chord. Although this makes playing leads and scales pretty difficult, open tuning opens up new possibilities for playing rhythms and chord progressions. Since the entire guitar is tuned to a chord in open tuning, you can play barre chords by using just one finger barred across all six strings. This frees up your other fingers to easily play suspensions and variations.

For open E tuning, start out in standard tuning and tune the 5th string up to B, the 4th string up to E, and the 1st string up to G#. Now the open string notes will be E - B_ - E_ - G#_ - B - E (all of the notes in an E major chord). The arrows are there to show you which direction to tune the string if you're starting out from standard tuning.

## Open E Tuning Rhythm

The staff below shows a simple progression you can play in open E tuning. It incorporates dead strums and the three chords E, G and A. You can barre across all six strings for the G and A chords using your third finger or your first and third fingers. Experiment with playing chords in open E tuning and decide which is most comfortable for you.

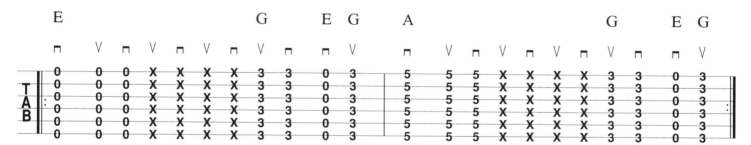

### Open G tuning:  D↓ - G↓ - D - G - B - D↓

### Open D tuning:  D↓ - A - D - F#↓ - A↓ - D↓

### Open E5 tuning #1:  E - B↑ - E↑ - B↑ - B - E

### Open E5 tuning #2:  E - E↓ - E↑ - B↑ - B - B↓

Open tuning also works great in combination with a capo or a slide. Here are a few more open tunings you can experiment with.

# Fingerpicking Pattern

Let's begin this section with a quick review of the fingerpicking technique and notation symbols from Chapter 5. When applying the fingerpicking technique to the guitar, pluck downward with your thumb and upward with your fingers. Thumb and fingers are labeled as p (thumb), i (index), m (middle), a (ring finger).

In the following exercise, fret and hold each chord and pick out the notes in the order shown on the tab staff. Use the letters underneath to show you which right hand fingers to use. As you get comfortable with the fingerpicking technique, try combining it with a capo and some of the open tunings from the previous lesson.

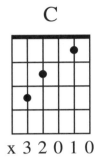
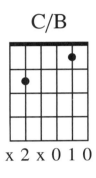
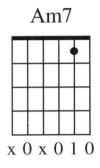

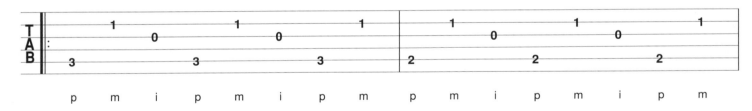

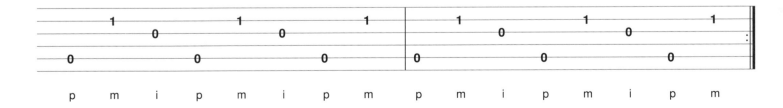

64

# Lead Techniques

## Slides

In the following example, slide from note to note without lifting your finger off the fretboard. The "S" above the staff indicates a slide and the line between the notes shows the direction of the slide (up or down the neck). If there is a slur connecting two or more notes, pick only the first note and slide directly to the next without picking. You can perform slides using any finger, but you'll probably use first and third finger slides more often. This exercise is played using the first position A minor pentatonic scale. After you get this down, try using the slide technique in other positions as well.

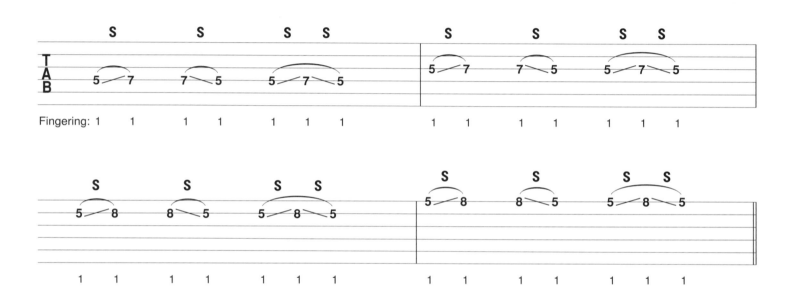

## Vibrato

Vibrato is the small, fast shaking of a note. Vibrato is indicated by a squiggly line above the staff, extending out from a note. While sustaining a note, shake your finger slightly and "dig in" to the note to slightly vibrate the pitch and give it more expression. Vibrato can also be applied while bending.

# Acoustic Slapping

While playing fingerstyle (without a pick), you can add a percussive, rhythmic feel to a chord progression by slapping the strings with your thumb. In the exercise below, fret the G chord in the first measure and follow the p-i-m-a right hand fingering, paying attention to where the rhythmic slaps occur in the progression.

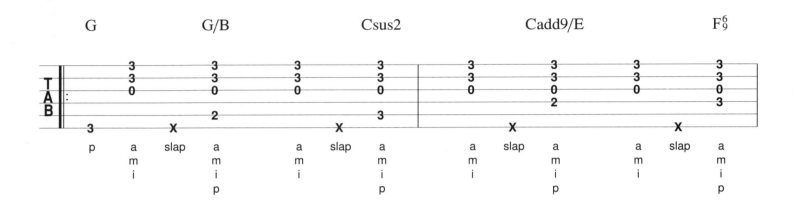

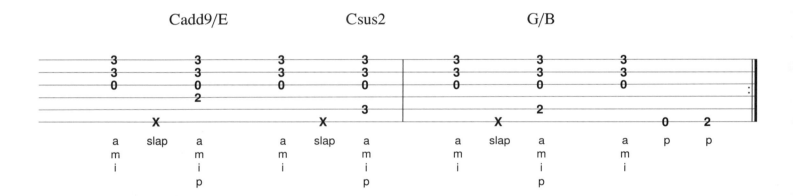

## Quick Quote!

"When you strum a guitar you have everything - rhythm, bass, lead and melody."

- David Gilmore / Pink Floyd

# Full Blues Lead

Here's an example of a solo that can be played over the shuffle blues rhythm you've just learned. This solo incorporates bends, hammer ons and pull offs in a variety of positions. The riff in the first measure is one of the most commonly used blues riffs; it can be heard in countless blues guitar solos. After you've got this solo down, try to create your own using the different lead techniques and all five positions of the A minor pentatonic scales.

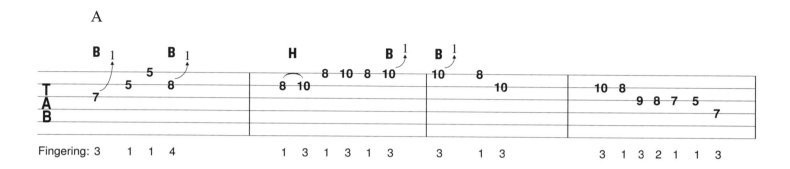

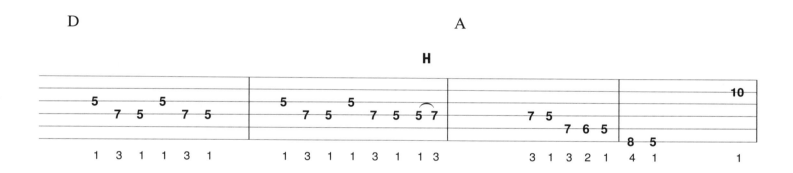

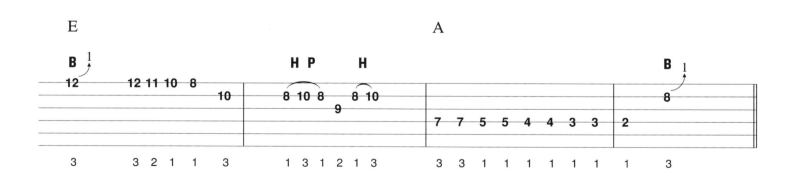

# House of the Rising Sun

Now it's time to have some fun! Here's a popular standard for acoustic guitar using all basic open chords. The timing (or meter) for this song is in three and can be counted as 3/4 or 6/8 time. Listen to the CD track to get a feel for the rhythm. Memorize the strumming pattern indicated above the first measure and use this pattern throughout the song. Keep your strumming arm loose and relaxed and make sure you change chords smoothly and efficiently. The key of the song is A minor, so you can also have fun playing your own solos over the progression using the A minor pentatonic scales we've used in the previous lessons.

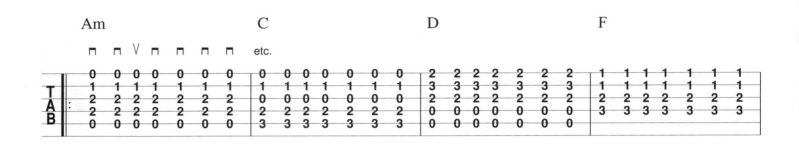

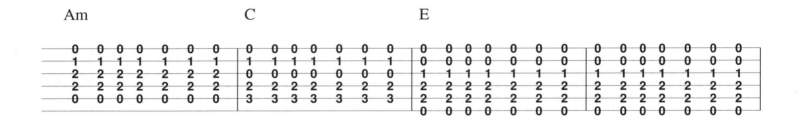

# Natural Minor Scales

Many modern Rock and Blues players have incorporated the use of full natural minor scales into their soloing. The pentatonic scales you've already learned are abbreviated versions of the regular major and minor scales. The pentatonic scales contain five notes; the natural minor scale contains seven notes. The word "natural" refers to the fact that the scale is in its original unaltered state. The natural minor scale can be used to create more complex and interesting melodies.

Below are the five basic positions of the B natural minor scale shown ascending and descending. The root notes have all been circled on the staff and scale diagrams.

## 1st Position B Minor Scale

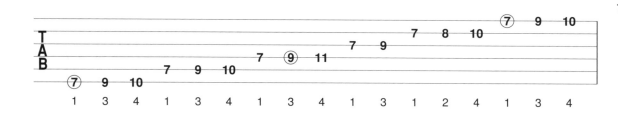

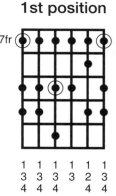

1st position

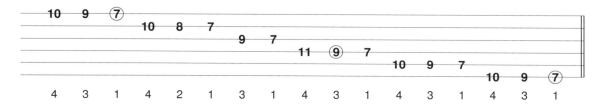

## 2nd Position B Minor Scale

2nd position

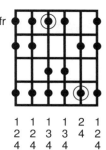

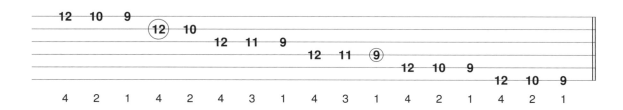

69

## 3rd Position B Minor Scale

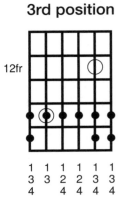

3rd position

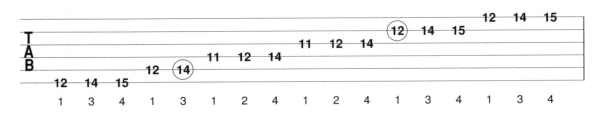

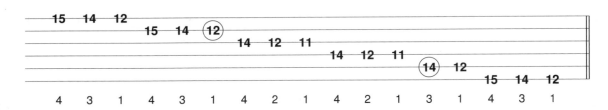

## 4th Position B Minor Scale

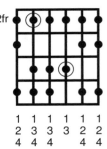

4th position

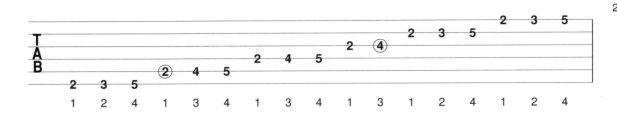

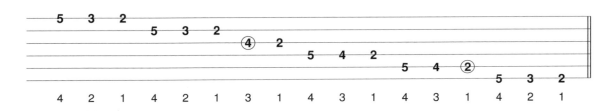

## 5th Position B Minor Scale

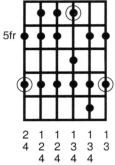

5th position

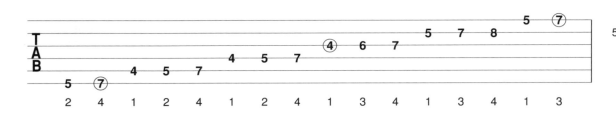

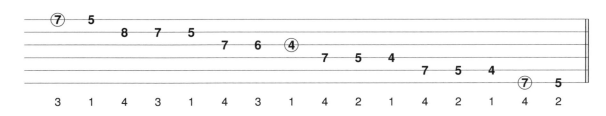

70

# Natural Minor Triplet Lead Pattern

Here is the 1st position A natural minor scale played in groups of three notes, or triplets. This pattern is similar to the triplet lead pattern we used for the minor pentatonic scales. Play through the scale in groups of three notes, with each group of three beginning on the next successive scale degree. Each measure in the exercise below contains one triplet for reading convenience. Practice along with a metronome and keep the timing even and steady. Count "one - two - three, one - two - three" or "one trip-let, two trip-let" out loud to get the triplet feel in your head.

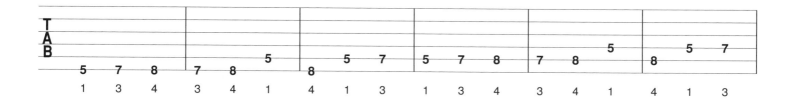

```
System 1
E|-5--7--8--7--8--8--8-------------------------------|
A|----------------5-----5--7--5--7--8--7--8----8-----|
D|--------------------------------------5--------5-7-|
 fingers: 1 3 4 | 3 4 1 | 4 1 3 | 1 3 4 | 3 4 1 | 4 1 3

System 2
D|-5--7--9--7--9--9--9-------------------------------|
G|----------------5-----5--7--5--7--7----------------|
B|-----------------------------------5-----5-6--5-6-8|
 fingers: 1 3 4 | 3 4 1 | 4 1 3 | 1 3 1 | 3 1 2 | 1 2 4

System 3
B|-6--8-----8-------------------------------8-----8-6|
e|-------5-----5--7--5--7--8--8--7--5--7--5----5-----|
 fingers: 2 4 1 | 4 1 3 | 1 3 4 | 4 3 1 | 3 1 4 | 1 4 2

System 4
B|-8--6--5--6--5--5----------------------------------|
G|----------------7-----7--5--7--5--------5----------|
D|--------------------------------9-----9--7--9--7--5|
 fingers: 4 2 1 | 2 1 3 | 1 3 1 | 3 1 4 | 1 4 3 | 4 3 1
```

The purpose of playing these lead patterns is for you to get used to phrasing the scales in many different ways, instead of just playing them forwards and backwards. If you think of the scales and chords as your alphabet and vocabulary, then practicing lead patterns is similar to honing your writing or typing skills. The more control you have over scale patterns, the easier it will be for you to play creative and interesting melodies. Below is the 2nd position of the natural minor scale triplet pattern. After you've learned this one, play the remaining three positions using this pattern as well.

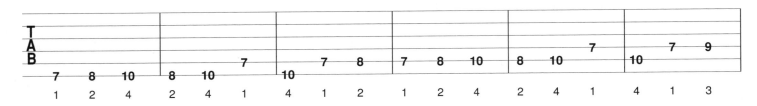

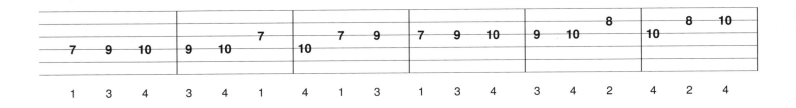

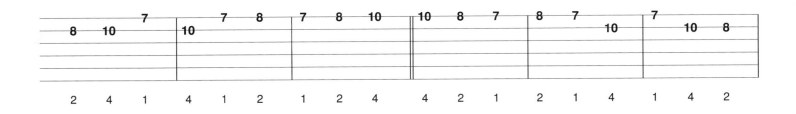

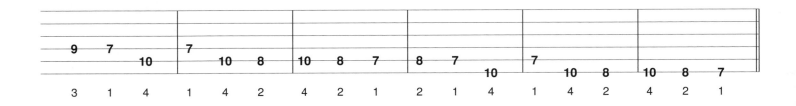

72

# Minor Seventh Rhythm

In this lesson, we'll introduce some new chords and show you a progression in the key of B minor. Once you've got the rhythm down, you can try soloing over the rhythm track using all of the B natural minor scale positions.

These minor seventh chords have slightly different fingerings from the ones you've already learned. For the Bm7 chord, deaden the 5th string by slightly tilting the second finger on your left hand to mute the string. Use the same technique while playing the Em7 chord to mute the 4th string with your first finger. Pay close attention to the DVD lesson for important tips.

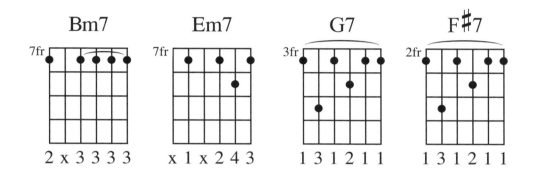

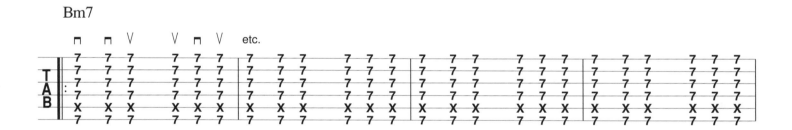

The following improvised lead example has been transcribed in tab for your reference. Play through the riffs to get some ideas on how to use the B natural minor scales and all of the lead techniques to create your own melodic solos in minor keys.

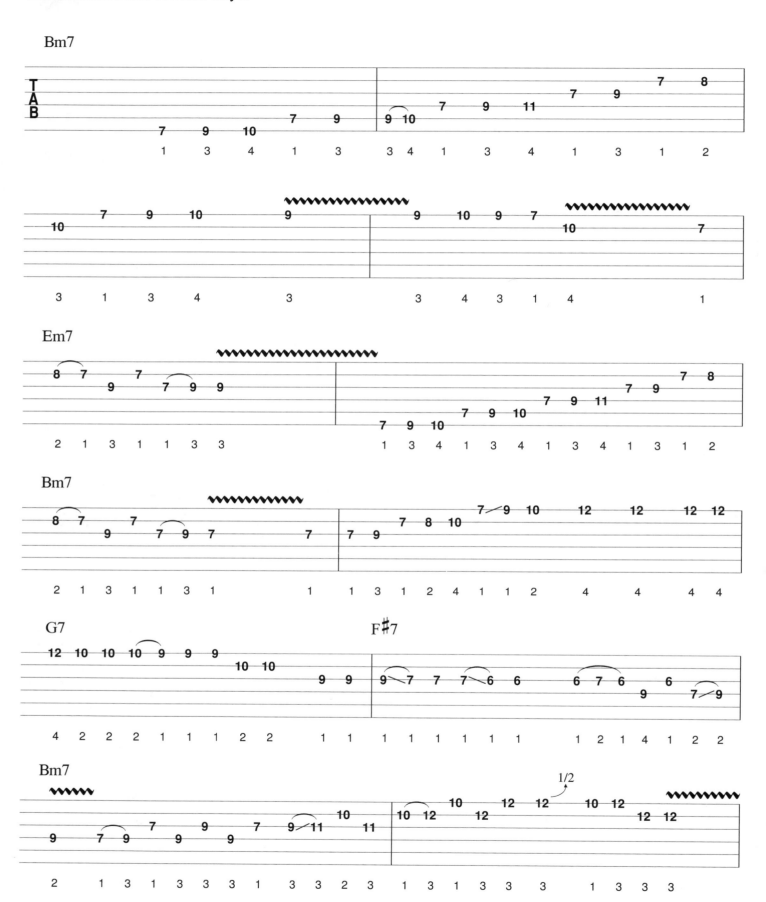

**Bm7**

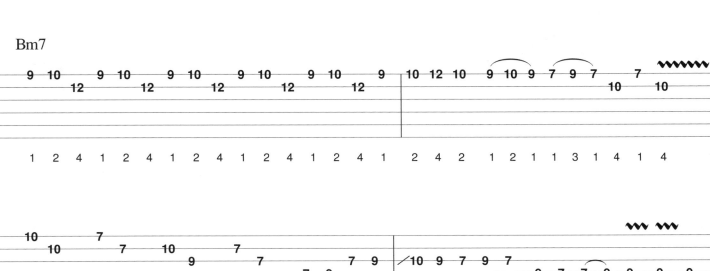

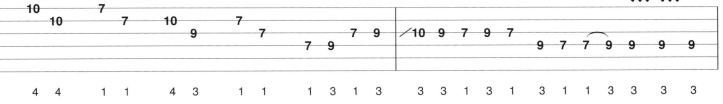

**Em7**

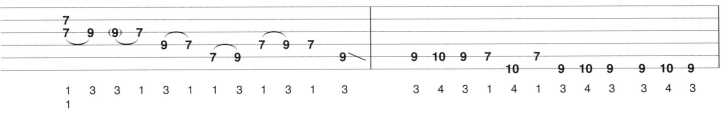

**Bm7**

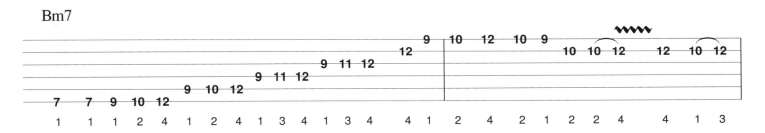

**G7**                                    **F#7**

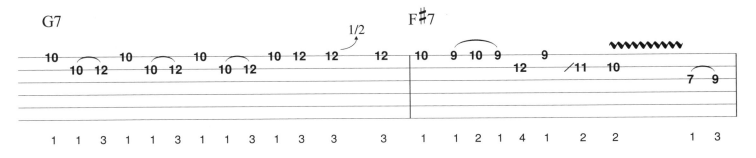

**Bm7**

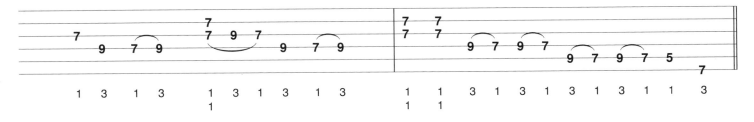

# Rockin' the Blues - Dead Strums

Here's a rock blues progression that incorporates dead strums, performed by muting the strings with your left hand and strumming the muted strings. These muted notes are shown using x's on the tab staff below. Pay attention to the picking symbols above the staff to show you when to up strum or down strum. This particular example places dead strums between most of the normal strums, giving the progression more of percussive sound and a rock feel. This example is also played in a shuffle feel. Jam along with the backing track until you have the groove, then try soloing over the progression using the A minor pentatonic scale in every position.

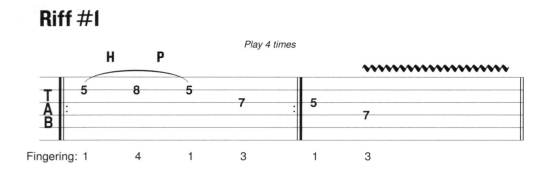

# Blues Riffs That Will Make Yo Mama Scream Part 2

Now let's add another set of blues riffs to your bag of tricks. These riffs incorporate all of the lead techniques over several positions of the Am pentatonic scale. The last riff uses a double stop slide (sliding two notes at once). After mastering these riffs, try transposing them to other keys and positions on the fretboard.

### Riff #1

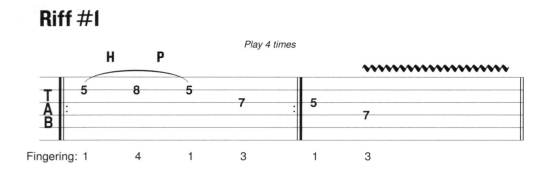

## Riff #2

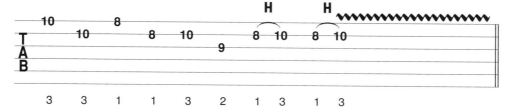

## Riff #3

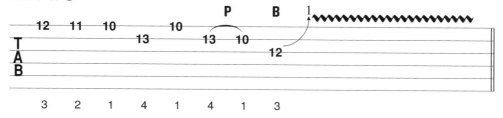

## Riff #4

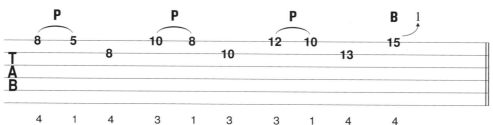

## Riff #5

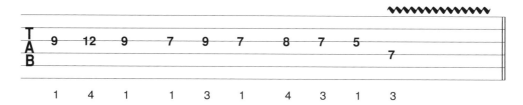

## Riff #6

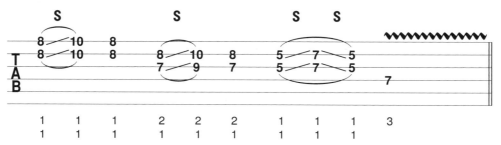

# Major Scale Triplet Lead Pattern

## 1st Position Triplet Lead Pattern

Here is the 1st position C major scale played in groups of three notes, or triplets. This pattern is similar to the triplet lead pattern we used for the minor pentatonic scales. Play through the scale in groups of three notes, with each group of three beginning on the next successive scale degree. Each measure below contains one triplet for reading convenience. Practice along with a metronome and keep the timing even and steady. Count "one - two - three, one - two - three" or "one trip-let, two trip-let" out loud to get the triplet feel in your head.

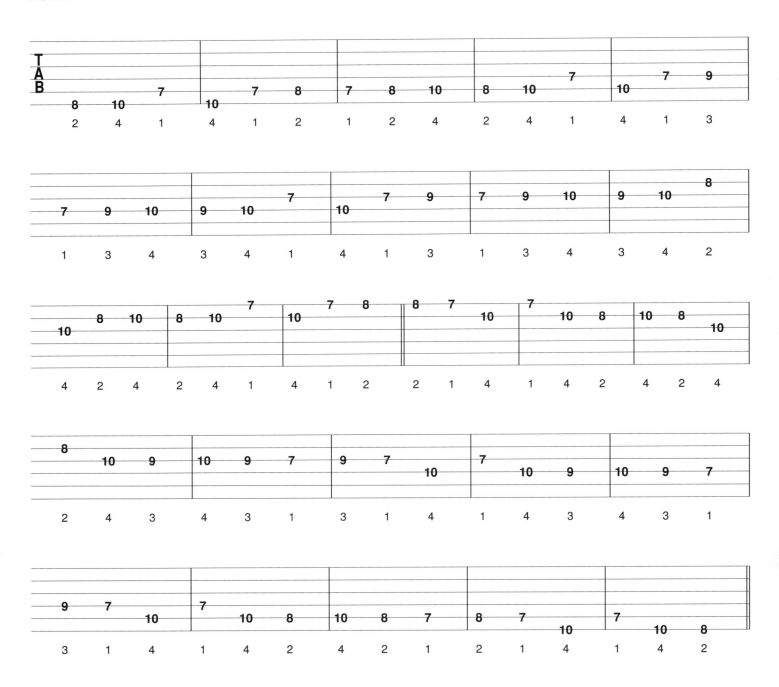

# 2nd Position Triplet Lead Pattern

The purpose of playing these lead patterns is for you to get used to phrasing the scales in many different ways, instead of just playing them forwards and backwards. If you think of the scales and chords as your alphabet and vocabulary, then practicing lead patterns is similar to honing your writing or typing skills. The more control you have over scale patterns, the easier it will be for you to play creative and interesting melodies. Below is the 2nd position of the major scale triplet pattern. After you've learned this one, play the remaining three positions using this pattern.

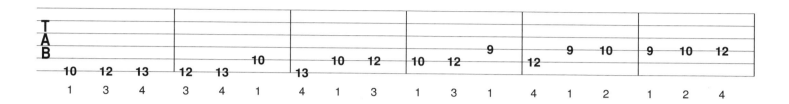

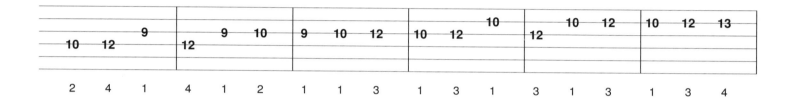

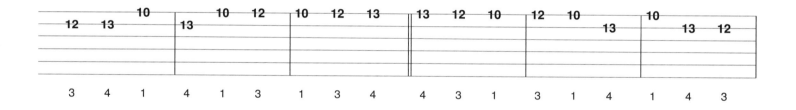

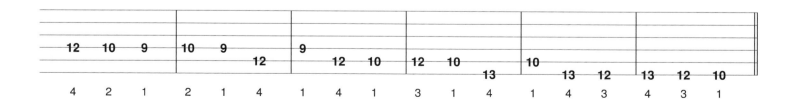

# Playing the Major Scale Over a Blues Progression

The backing track for this example is a slow blues that you can solo over using the C major scales. Play through this improvised example solo and follow along with the DVD and CD to get some ideas for creating melodic solos using the full major scale in all five positions.

This slow blues is in 6/8 time, a common time signature for this genre. It can be counted in groups of three, a triplet for each downbeat (one-two-three, one-two-three). The use of syncopation for many of the riffs gives the lead a spontaneous and soulful style

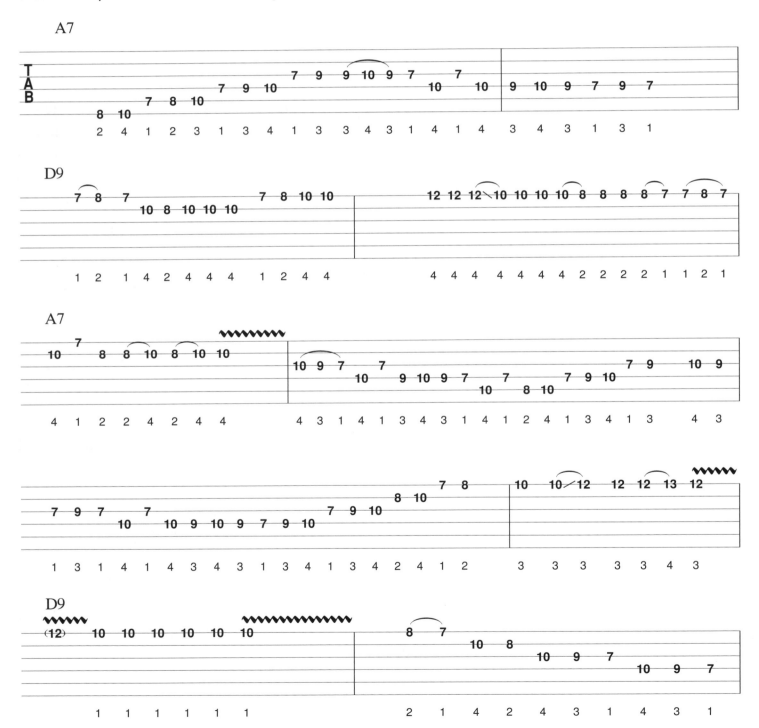

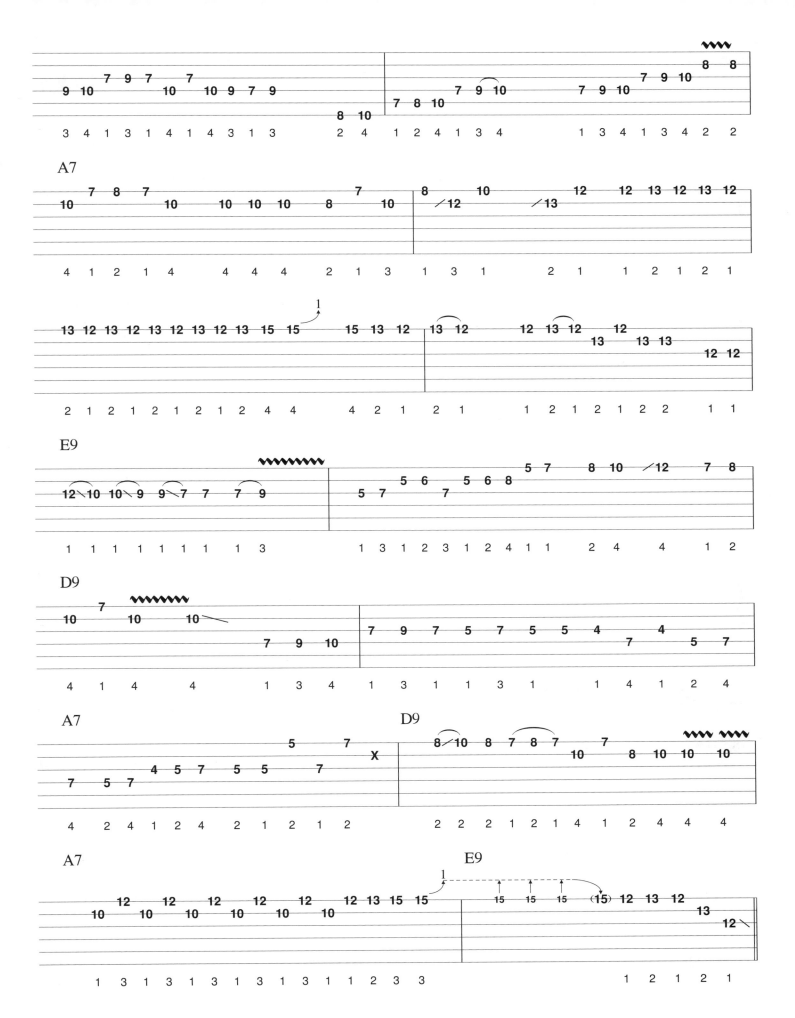

# 12 Bar Blues Progression

12-bar blues is a progression based on the I - IV - V chords that is 12 measures long. Most blues music is made up of 12-bar blues progressions; 12 measures of music that repeat throughout the song. This particular example combines barre chords and single notes in the key of A. The single notes at the end of each measure are played with the first and third fingers in the same position as each chord. Play along with the backing track to get the shuffle feel.

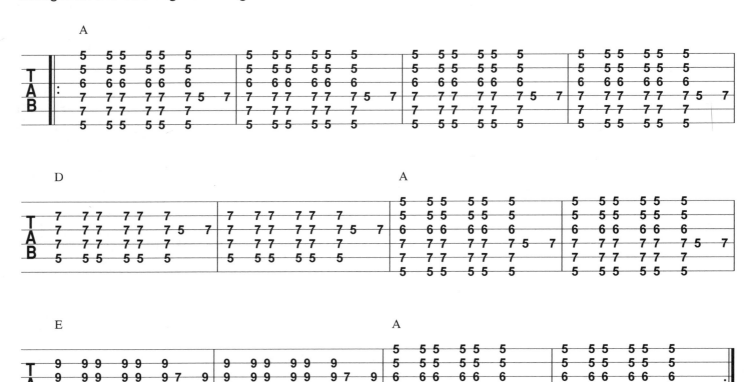

# 12 Bar Theory

Let's discuss the basic theory behind the 12 bar blues form. As we said before the 12 bar progression is commonly used in blues music. This progression is 12 bars or measures consisting of only the I, IV, and V chords of a given key. To determine which chords they are let's look at the notes of a one octave C Major Scale:

## C Major Scale – C D E F G A B C

Now let's add numeric degrees to the scale:

| C | D | E | F | G | A | B | C |
|---|---|---|---|---|---|---|---|
| I | II | III | IV | V | VI | VII | I |

If you look at the diagram above you will notice that the C is I, F is the IV, and G is the V. Commonly in blues we would take these three degrees and form Dominant 7th chords from them which would give us the C7, F7, and G7 Chords. However, if you want a Major or minor Blues, you could substitute either major or minor chords for these.

Now let's look at two commonly used forms of the 12 bar blues progression. One is called "Slow Changes" and the other is called "Fast Changes." The difference between slow and fast changes is the second measure. Slow changes is when the I chord is played for the first four measures. Fast changes is when the IV chord is played in place of the I chord in the second measure. Both of these have a distinct sound that is heard commonly in both Blues and Rock music.

## 12 Bar "Slow Changes"

| C7 | C7 | C7 | C7 |
|----|----|----|----|
| F7 | F7 | C7 | C7 |
| G7 | F7 | C7 | G7 |

## 12 Bar "Fast Changes"

| C7 | F7 | C7 | C7 |
|----|----|----|----|
| F7 | F7 | C7 | C7 |
| G7 | F7 | C7 | G7 |

# Open Chord Blues Progression in Em

The following progression uses some new open chord variations and suspensions. The chord diagrams show the fingerings for the chords used in this exercise. Notice that the fingering for the Em chord has been varied slightly in order to make it easier to change from chord to chord. Play along with the backing track and get the rhythm down. After you've learned the rhythm part, you can transpose the minor pentatonic scale positions to Em and solo over it. The five positions of the E minor pentatonic scale are also available on the Lesson Support Site. When creating your own solos, use bends, hammer ons, pull offs, slides and vibrato to add personal expression to your playing.

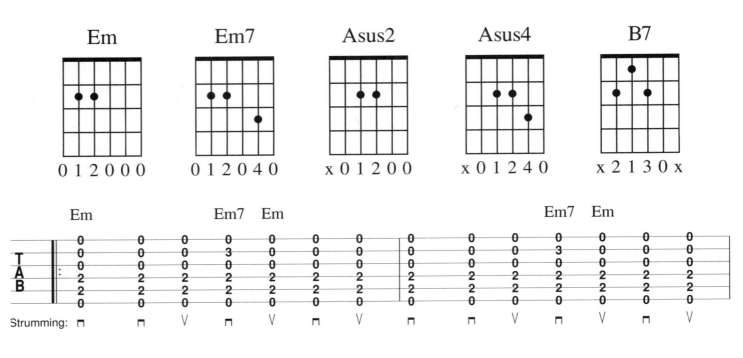

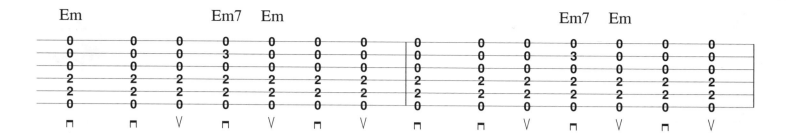

## Quick Quote!

"Blues is easy to play, but hard to feel."

- Jimi Hendrix

# Blues Scales - Key of E

The blues scale is a slight variation of the minor pentatonic scale. It contains one extra note between the 4th and 5th steps of the scale, called a passing tone. This particular passing tone is the flatted fifth of the scale, also known as the blues tri-tone. Using the blues tri-tone adds color and character to solos and riffs. This note is a chromatic passing tone because it passes from the 4th to the 5th steps of the scale in chromatic half steps. Passing tones are used to connect from note to note within a phrase and are generally not held for long durations.

The following five scale positions of the E blues scale are the same as the E minor pentatonic scale with the addition of the blues tri-tone. The x's in the scale diagrams to the right indicate where the blues tri-tones are played. Practice and memorize the E blues scale positions; we'll be using these scales to play solos in many of the following sections.

## 1st Position E Blues Scale

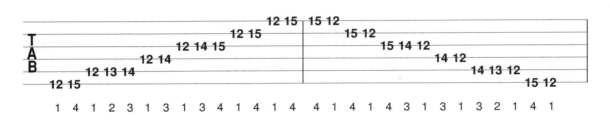

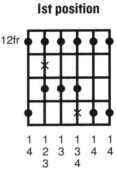

## 2nd Position E Blues Scale

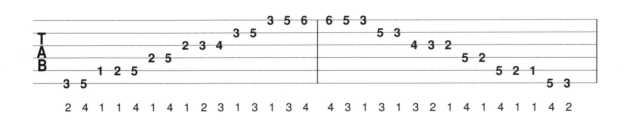

## 3rd Position E Blues Scale

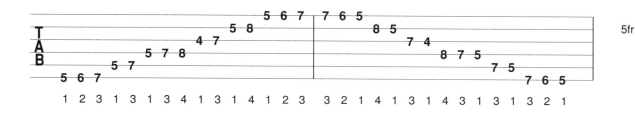
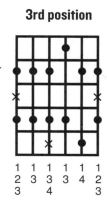

**3rd position**

## 4th Position E Blues Scale

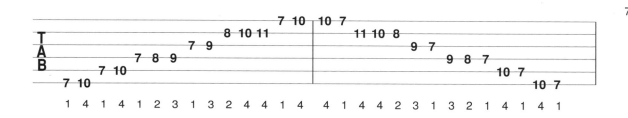
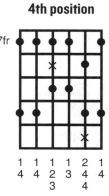

**4th position**

## 5th Position E Blues Scale

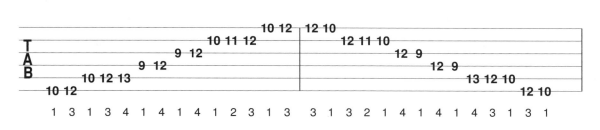
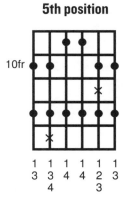

**5th position**

## Open Position E Blues Scale

The first position of the E blues scale can also be transposed one octave lower and played in open position. This particular scale position is used often in blues music. Playing in open position makes hammer ons, pull offs and trills very easy to perform, making this particular scale a favorite for many guitarists. To play any scale position an octave higher or lower, move the scale pattern 12 frets in the appropriate direction.

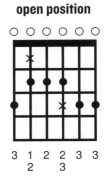

open position

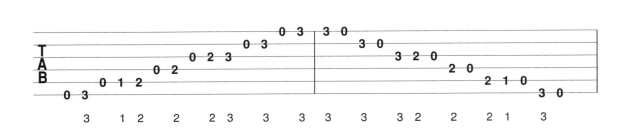

## Blues Scale Fretboard Diagram

The following fretboard diagram shows all of the notes in the E blues scales and how the positions overlap each other. The blues tri-tones are indicated by X's. Since the blues tri-tone is a passing tone within the minor pentatonic scale, the regular dots by themselves also indicate all of the notes of the E minor pentatonic scale. This is a very popular key for blues progressions and solos, so you should familiarize yourself with every position of the scale.

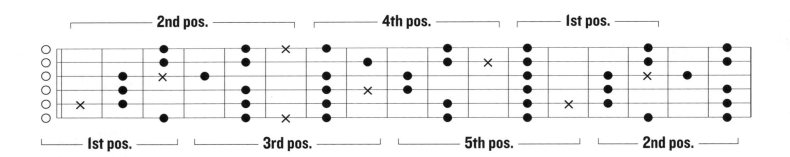

# Open String Blues Rhythm in E

The following rhythm is a standard I - IV - V progression in E with a shuffle feel. The last two-measure phrase is a turnaround (a riff that brings you back around to the beginning of the progression). The riff should be played using alternate picking; let the notes ring out together. This particular turnaround uses a descending chromatic riff leading back to the V (five) chord, B. Practice the rhythm along with the backing track, then improvise and solo over it using the E blues scale in various positions.

E

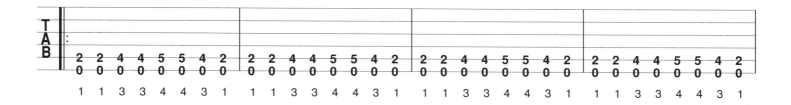

A                                                          E

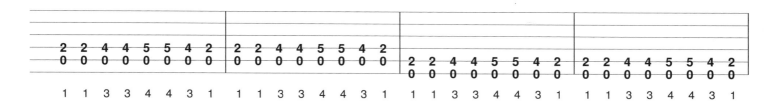

B                          A                      E                          B

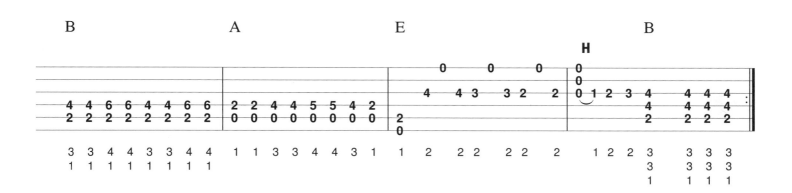

# Creating Leads and Melodies

Making up your own melodic leads is much easier than you'd think once you know your scales. In this lesson we'll use the A natural minor scales to show you how. Watch the video lesson for tips on how to easily create your own melodies. Begin slowly by just playing forwards and backwards within the scale. Use your ear to help find the notes that sound good against the rhythm track. Some of the most recognizable melodic leads are based around a few simple notes or a repeated riff. Here's an example of some simple melodies using the 1st position A natural minor scale. Take a quick look through this easy solo to give you some ideas, then jam along with the rhythm track and come up with your own.

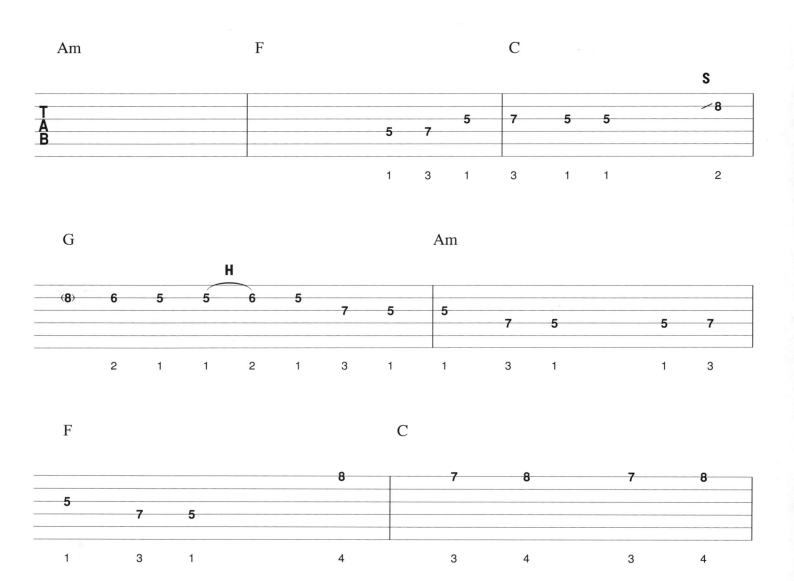

G                                    Am

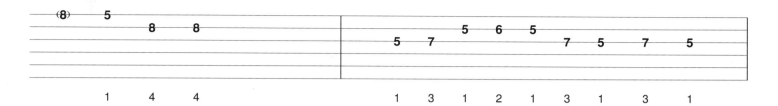

F                                    C

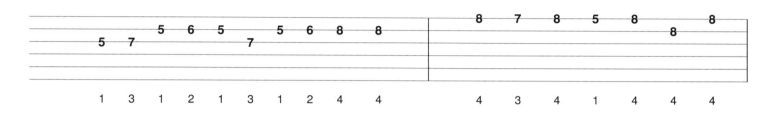

G                                    Am

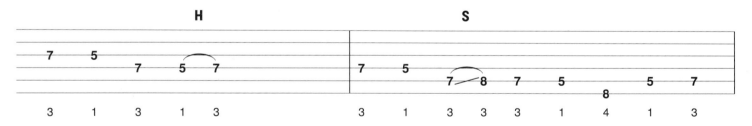

F                                    C

G                                    Am

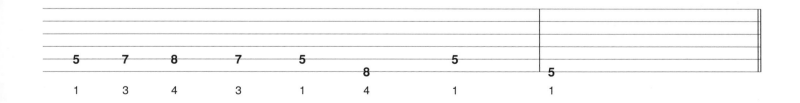

# Sixteenth Note Scale Pattern

This lesson will introduce a new scale pattern designed to help build coordination and diversify your phrasing when using the major and minor scales.

## Sixteenth Note C Major Scale Pattern

Sixteenth notes are four notes played within one beat. Sixteenth notes can be counted as groups of four notes: "one, two, three, four, one, two, three, four." You can also count sixteenth notes as "one-e-and-a, two-e-and-a," to help keep track of what number beat you are on. The following sixteenth note scale pattern ascends and descends through the 1st position of the C major scale in groups of four notes; the bar lines have been placed after each grouping for reading convenience and the left hand fingering is indicated below the tab staff. Practice slowly with a metronome and gradually build up speed, remembering to use consistent, alternate picking. Once you've got the phrasing down, try playing all five positions of the major scale using this pattern.

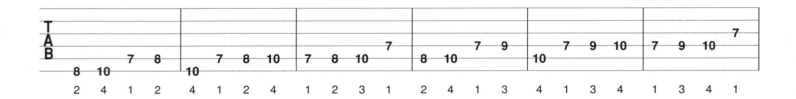

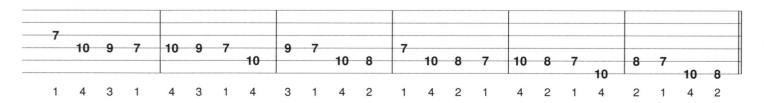

# Sixteenth Note B Minor Scale Pattern

Now let's take that sixteenth note pattern and use it to play the 1st position B natural minor scale. Watch your left hand fingering and make sure you use alternate picking to build speed and keep your timing steady and smooth. When you've got it down using the 1st position, transpose the pattern to all of the remaining positions of the natural minor scale.

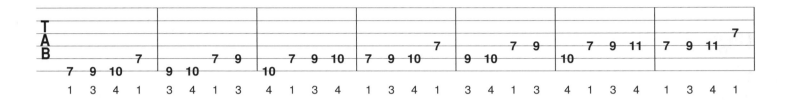

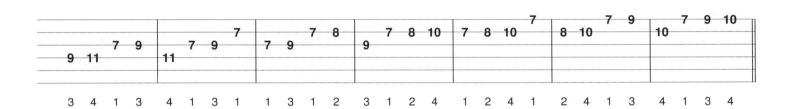

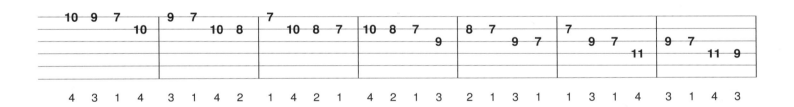

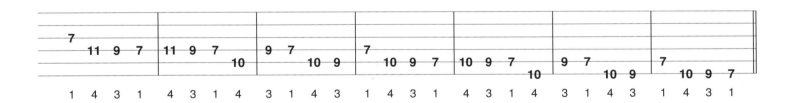

# Workout Section

The following workout section contains a series of exclusive Rock House finger exercises designed to strengthen specific areas of your playing technique. All of these exercises should be practiced along with a metronome. Start out slowly and build speed gradually. Use alternate picking when required and always be sure to use proper fret hand technique.

## Finger Crusher

The finger crusher is a left hand workout that will make your fingers stronger and faster. Each section of the exercise starts with a two-string pattern from the minor pentatonic scale. Play it four times in position, then move the pattern chromatically (one fret at a time) up the neck to the 12th fret and chromatically back down to where you started at the 5th fret. Your hand will probably get sore and tired before you're even halfway through the exercise, but that just means you're doing it right and getting a great workout. Try to keep time with the metronome and make it your goal to get through the entire exercise without stopping.

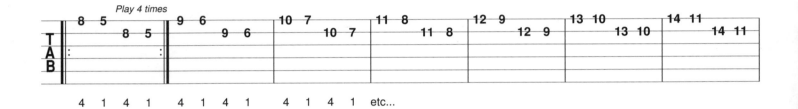

94

*Play 4 times*

```
|| 7  5           || 8  6          | 9  7          | 10  8         | 11  9         | 12 10         | 13 11         |
||       7  5     ||      8  6     |      9  7     |      10  8    |      11  9    |      12 10    |      13 11    |
```

3  1  3  1     3  1  3  1     3  1  3  1     etc...

```
| 14 12         | 13 11         | 12 10         | 11  9         | 10  8         | 9  7          | 8  6          | 7  5          |
|      14 12    |      13 11    |      12 10    |      11  9    |      10  8    |      9  7     |      8  6     |      7  5     |
```

*Play 4 times*

```
|| 7  5           || 8  6          | 9  7          | 10  8         | 11  9         | 12 10         | 13 11         |
||       7  5     ||      8  6     |      9  7     |      10  8    |      11  9    |      12 10    |      13 11    |
```

3  1  3  1     3  1  3  1     3  1  3  1     etc...

```
| 14 12         | 13 11         | 12 10         | 11  9         | 10  8         | 9  7          | 8  6          | 7  5          |
|      14 12    |      13 11    |      12 10    |      11  9    |      10  8    |      9  7     |      8  6     |      7  5     |
```

*Play 4 times*

```
|| 7  5           || 8  6          | 9  7          | 10  8         | 11  9         | 12 10         | 13 11         |
||       8  5     ||      9  6     |      10  7    |      11  8    |      12  9    |      13 10    |      14 11    |
```

3  1  4  1     3  1  4  1     3  1  4  1     etc...

```
| 14 12         | 13 11         | 12 10         | 11  9         | 10  8         | 9  7          | 8  6          | 7  5          ||
|      15 12    |      14 11    |      13 10    |      12  9    |      11  8    |      10  7    |      9  6     |      8  5     ||
```

# One Hand Rolls

Here's an exercise designed to strengthen your left hand using a series of hammer ons and pull offs. All of the notes should be produced by the left hand only; don't use the pick at all. Watch the DVD lesson for tips on how to use your right hand to mute the other strings. Once you've got the technique down, practice One Hand Rolls on the other strings.

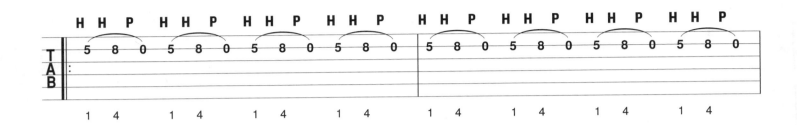

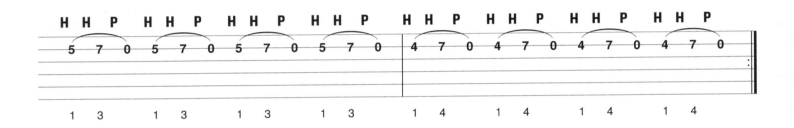

## Quick Tip!

### USE A METRONOME

*One of the most important tools in your practice arsenal is your metronome. Use it to ensure that you stay in time and on the beat, whether you're practicing scales, progressions or finger exercises. If you get comfortable playing along with a metronome, playing with a band will be a breeze!*

# The Killer!!

This exercise is designed to work on your left hand coordination. Use consistent alternate picking throughout. Play through the first measure slowly until you memorize the pattern. Notice that all four fingers of the left hand are used in succession. For each consecutive measure, the pattern moves down one string. The bottom two tab staffs show the pattern in reverse.

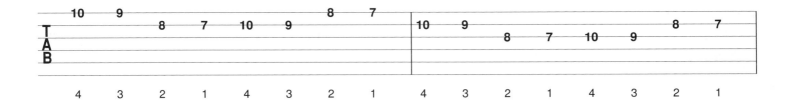

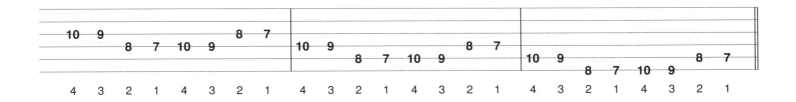

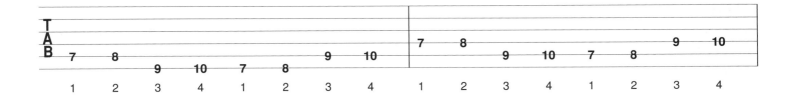

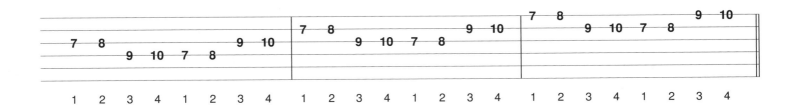

# Arpeggio Sweep Technique

An arpeggio is defined as the notes of a chord played separately. Major arpeggios contain three different name notes: the root note (which is the same note as the arpeggio or chord's letter name), the third (which is the third scale step and letter name up from the root note), and the fifth (the fifth scale step and letter name up from the root note). Full major chords on the guitar are actually groups of root notes, thirds and fifths in different octaves that your hand can reach within that position. Once you know the theory behind which individual notes belong in the chord and where they are on the fretboard, you can create your own chords. More information on arpeggio and chord theory can be found on the Lesson Support Site. The first arpeggio example below uses alternate picking.

## Alternate Picking

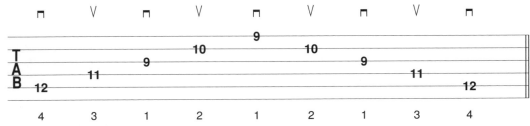

Now try the same A major arpeggio using the sweep picking technique. Sweep picking is performed by dragging the pick across the strings in one smooth, flowing motion. In the example below, sweep downward with the pick across the ascending part of the arpeggio, then sweep back up across the strings with the pick using the same smooth motion. Sweep picking is a very useful technique for playing fast arpeggio runs. The downward sweep picking motion is also referred to as raking. This technique may be indicated in music and tablature using the word "rake" followed by a dashed line.

## Sweep Picking

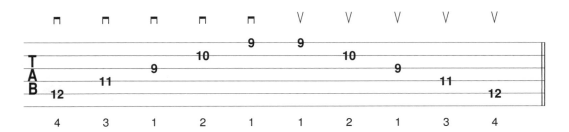

# Advanced Bending Techniques

## Half Step Bend

Half step bends are especially useful for soloing with blues scales. Train your ear to hear the difference between whole step and half step bends; eventually your fingers will instinctively know how much to bend the strings to achieve the correct pitches.

## Ghost Bend

Ghost bends (sometimes referred to as pre-bends) are performed by bending the note to the proper pitch before striking the note. In this example, pre-bend the note a half step and then pick the note and gradually release the note to its original pitch.

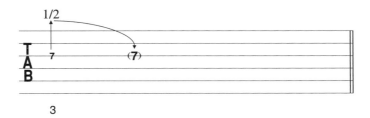

## Double Pump Bend

You also bend and release the same note repeatedly without picking it again. The following example uses a bend-release-bend-release pattern. This technique can be used in a variety of ways.

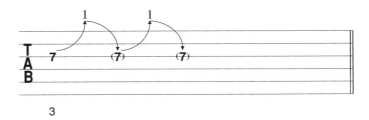

## Scream Bend

To perform the following scream bend, pick both notes simultaneously and bend just the lower note up a whole step. Keep the higher note stationary and allow it to ring out along with the bend.

# Blues Lead in E

Here's an example of a blues lead that can be played over the Open String Blues Rhythm in E from earlier in this section. Listen to the backing track to get the rhythm and the phrasing. This solo incorporates many different types of bends as well as hammer ons, pull offs, and slides.

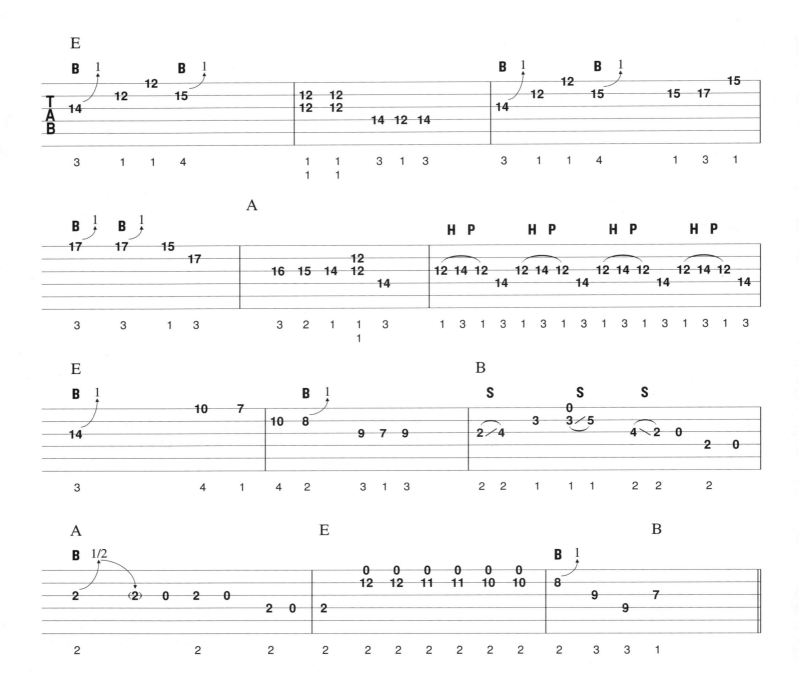

# Bi-Dextral Hammer Ons

This technique introduces the right hand tap, which requires you to reach over to the neck with your right hand and hammer on the note using your right hand index or middle finger. After tapping the note, pull off with your right hand finger to the lower notes on the neck that should be fretted with your left hand fingers. The "R" above the tab staff indicates a right hand tap. This technique allows you to hammer on and pull off full arpeggios and other wide interval phrases very quickly. Right hand tapping was made popular by Eddie Van Halen, who used tapping throughout many of his famous solos.

If you tap with your middle finger, you can keep the pick in position in your hand. If you feel more comfortable tapping with your index finger, you can use a technique called "palming the pick" where you tuck the pick under your middle finger to get it out of the way. After playing the riff, bring it back into position to go back to regular picking.

The following riff is an example of what you can do with bi-dextral hammer ons. Once you're comfortable with the technique, experiment with it at different frets and on different strings. You can also do other fun things with this technique, such as bending a note in your left hand and then tapping a note above it while holding the bend. This bend and tap technique was made popular by Billy Gibbons.

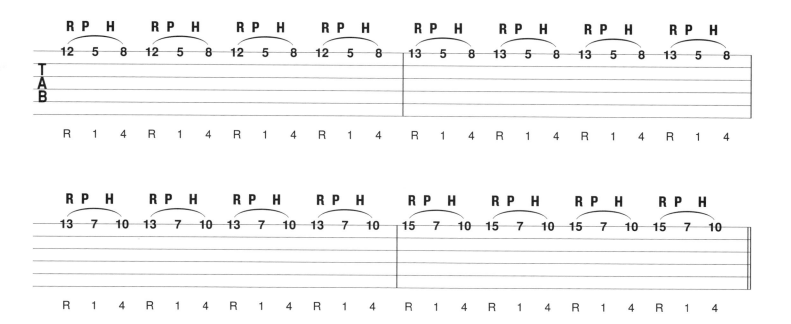

# Multi-Position Lead Pattern

This lead pattern uses the A minor pentatonic scale and is played across three positions of the scale. It demonstrates various ways to switch from position to position. Play through the entire example along with the metronome and start out slowly until you're comfortable with the position changes. After you learn this example, start experimenting with every scale and discover some new ways to switch between each position.

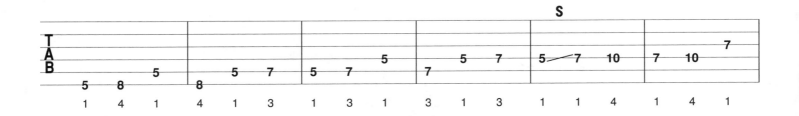

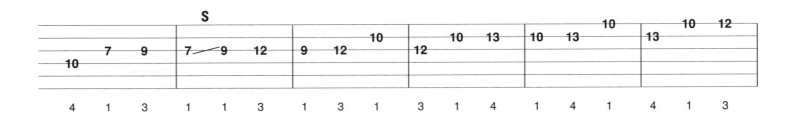

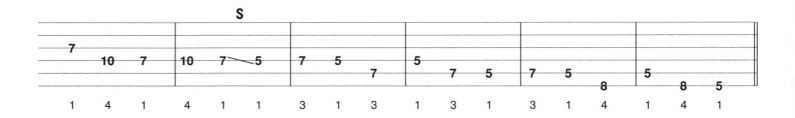

# Advanced Blues Jazz Chords

The following chords are extensions of the regular major and minor chords. The 9th, major 7th and minor 7th chords are commonly used in blues to achieve a jazzier sound. These are all moveable chords and can be transposed to any key.

### A9

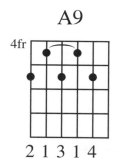

4fr

2 1 3 1 4

### A9

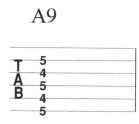

```
T  5
A  4
B  5
   4
   5
```

### D9

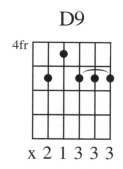

4fr

x 2 1 3 3 3

### D9

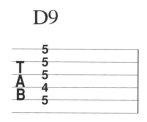

```
T  5
A  5
B  5
   4
   5
```

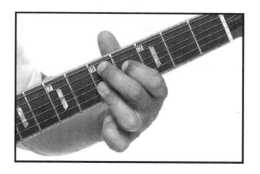

## Am7

5fr

1 3 1 1 1 1

## Am7

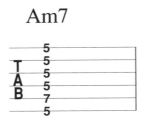

```
  5
  5
T 5
A 5
B 7
  5
```

## Dm7

5fr

x 1 3 1 2 1

## Dm7

```
  5
  6
T 5
A 7
B 5
```

## Amaj7

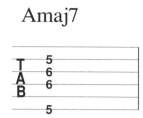

5fr

1 x 3 4 2 x

## Amaj7

```
T    5
A    6
B    6
     5
```

## Dmaj7

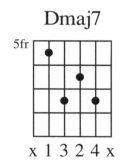

5fr

x 1 3 2 4 x

## Dmaj7

```
T    7
A    6
B    7
     5
```

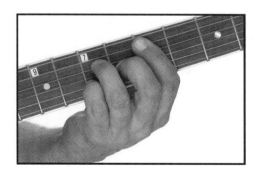

# The Jazz Blues Fuze

This jazz blues fuze rhythm is another example of a 12-bar blues progression, the most popular progression used in blues music. This progression uses all 9th chords and is an example of a slow, jazzy blues. The rhythm is played with a straight feel in 6/8 time (six eighth notes per measure). The strumming pattern is indicated above the staff. Count along with the backing track to get the rhythm in your head. The rhythmic feel is in groups of three. Follow the slow blues drum beat and accent your strumming on the downbeats (the first and fourth eighth notes of each measure). When you get the feel down and you're ready to try soloing over the progression, transpose the blues scale positions to the key of A and use them to play leads along with the backing track.

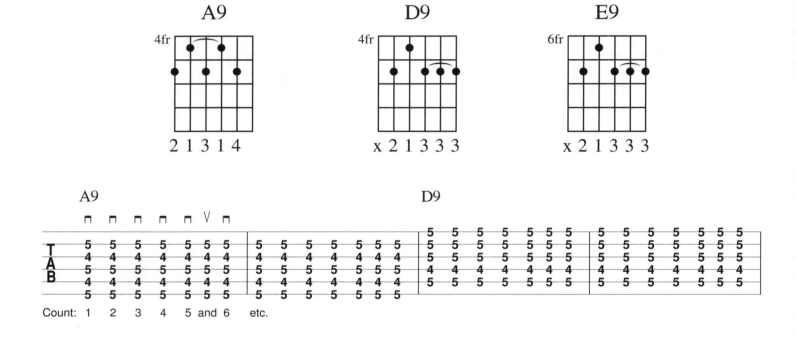

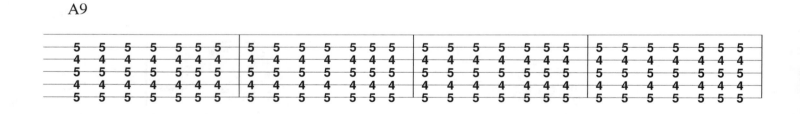

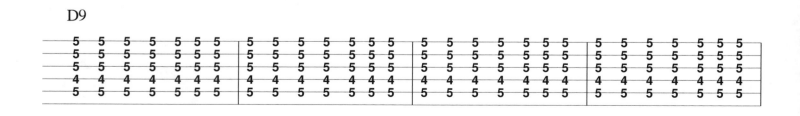

106

A9

```
|5  5  5  5  5 5 5 |5  5  5  5  5 5 5 |5  5  5  5  5 5 5 |5  5  5  5  5 5 5 |
|4  4  4  4  4 4 4 |4  4  4  4  4 4 4 |4  4  4  4  4 4 4 |4  4  4  4  4 4 4 |
|5  5  5  5  5 5 5 |5  5  5  5  5 5 5 |5  5  5  5  5 5 5 |5  5  5  5  5 5 5 |
|4  4  4  4  4 4 4 |4  4  4  4  4 4 4 |4  4  4  4  4 4 4 |4  4  4  4  4 4 4 |
|5  5  5  5  5 5 5 |5  5  5  5  5 5 5 |5  5  5  5  5 5 5 |5  5  5  5  5 5 5 |
```

E9                                         D9

```
|7  7  7  7  7 7 7 |7  7  7  7  7 7 7 |5  5  5  5  5 5 5 |5  5  5  5  5 5 5 |
|7  7  7  7  7 7 7 |7  7  7  7  7 7 7 |5  5  5  5  5 5 5 |5  5  5  5  5 5 5 |
|7  7  7  7  7 7 7 |7  7  7  7  7 7 7 |5  5  5  5  5 5 5 |5  5  5  5  5 5 5 |
|6  6  6  6  6 6 6 |6  6  6  6  6 6 6 |4  4  4  4  4 4 4 |4  4  4  4  4 4 4 |
|7  7  7  7  7 7 7 |7  7  7  7  7 7 7 |5  5  5  5  5 5 5 |5  5  5  5  5 5 5 |
```

A9                  D9                  A9                  E9

```
                   |5  5  5  5  5 5 5 |                   |7  7  7  7  7 7 7 |
|5  5  5  5  5 5 5 |5  5  5  5  5 5 5 |                   |7  7  7  7  7 7 7 |
|4  4  4  4  4 4 4 |5  5  5  5  5 5 5 |5  5  5  5  5 5 5 |7  7  7  7  7 7 7 |
|5  5  5  5  5 5 5 |4  4  4  4  4 4 4 |4  4  4  4  4 4 4 |6  6  6  6  6 6 6 |
|4  4  4  4  4 4 4 |5  5  5  5  5 5 5 |5  5  5  5  5 5 5 |7  7  7  7  7 7 7 |
|5  5  5  5  5 5 5 |                   |4  4  4  4  4 4 4 |                  |
                                      |5  5  5  5  5 5 5 |
```

# Lead Techniques

## Rakes

A rake is a series of muted adjacent strings picked before a note. Pick downward across the strings in one sweeping motion while deadening them with your left hand. In this example, the x's represent the rake leading into the notes on the 1st string. Rakes are commonly used to accent a bend.

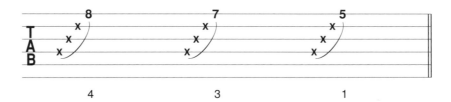

# Pick & Finger

This technique is especially popular with blues and country players. Hold the pick as you normally would, then use your middle and ring fingers to pick additional notes. You can achieve quick jumps from low to high notes using this technique. In the first example, the notes are played together by down picking with the pick and simultaneously plucking upward with the middle finger. Use a pinching motion with the pick and middle finger to pluck the notes together. The left hand fingering is indicated under the staff. Leave your first finger barred across the first three strings while reaching with your third and fourth fingers for the other notes along the 3rd string. Once you get the idea, try coming up with your own riffs and incorporate this style into your improvisational repertoire.

```
T      12      12      12      12      12
A      12      14      15      14      12
B


       1       1       1       1       1
       1       3       4       3       1
```

Here's another example using the pick and finger technique. The notes are picked individually in this exercise, alternating between the pick and middle finger. After the initial slide at the beginning of the riff, leave your second finger stationary at the 9th fret on the 3rd string. All of the notes on the 3rd string are down picked using the pick. All of notes on the 1st and 2nd strings are plucked upward with the middle finger. After you have this technique down, try to use it in different scale positions and keys.

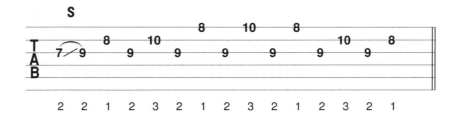

```
                              8      10      8
           S      8      10                        10      8
T      7/9     9      9       9      9       9   9
A
B


       2  2   1  2  3  2  1  2  3  2  1  2  3  2  1
```

# Advanced Blues Riffs

Now let's add some advanced blues riffs to your improvisational bag of tricks. These riffs are all recognizable and commonly used in blues solos and turnarounds. All five examples are shown here in the key of E. The first three riffs utilize the open strings, hammer ons, and pull offs.

In this first riff, all of the notes on the 3rd and 4th strings are fretted with the second finger or played open. This riff will develop coordination and help you to get comfortable using your second finger to perform slides and hammer ons.

### Riff # 1

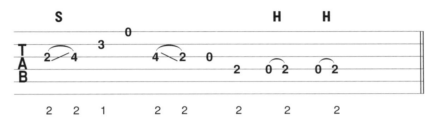

The first part of this next riff is a trill. A trill is a fast series of hammer ons and pull offs. Pick the open string and then rapidly hammer on and pull off at the 2nd fret repeatedly. The last part of the riff is a half step bend at the 3rd fret of the 6th string, followed by the open 6th string. This 3rd fret bend and open string combination is a very popular move and is commonly used in almost all styles of music.

### Riff # 2

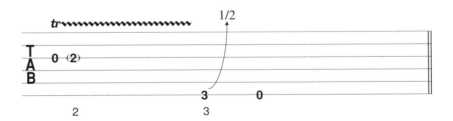

The third advanced blues riff uses a series of pull offs to the open 1st string. This example demonstrates how you can use open string pull offs to jump quickly from position to position.

## Riff # 3

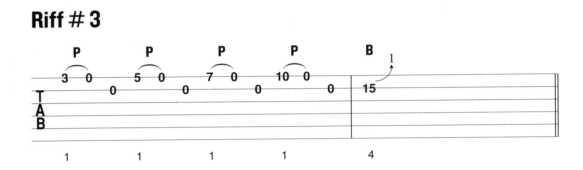

The fourth riff descends through the notes of the E blues scale, followed by a 3rd fret half step bend and open 6th string combination.

## Riff # 4

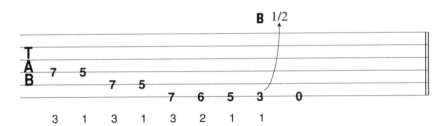

The last riff starts on a unison bend. Pick the notes together, bending the lower note until its pitch is in unison with the higher note. The next bend is a half step bend with the first finger at the 12th fret. Both of these bending techniques are very popular and widely used.

## Riff # 5

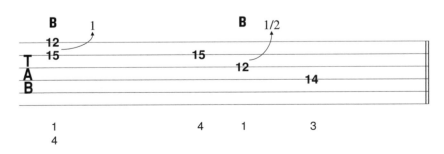

# Skipping Strings

This is another blues technique using the pick and finger method. When fretting the notes, use your second finger for all of the notes along the 3rd string. Alternate between your pick and middle finger to pluck the notes. The riff is shown ascending and then descending. Try this technique at different speeds and in different rhythms.

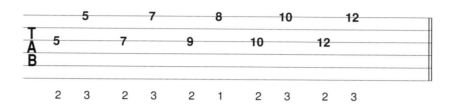

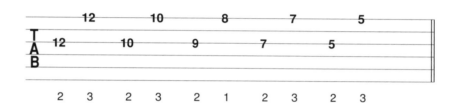

## Quick Quote!

"Between sets I'd sneak over to the black places to hear blues musicians. It got to the point where I was making my living at white clubs and having my fun at the other places."

- Stevie Ray Vaughan

# The C Major Pentatonic Scale

The key of C major is the relative major to the key of A minor. A minor and C major are relative keys because they both contain the same notes. When playing in A minor, A is the root note; when playing in C major, C is the root note. The following 5 scale positions are the exact same scale fingerings as the A minor pentatonic scales from Chapter 2, however the root note is now going to be C. The root notes are circled on the tab staff, and are shown as open dots on the scale diagrams. Memorize where the root notes are in every scale position in order to solo in C major.

## 1st Position C Major Pentatonic Scale

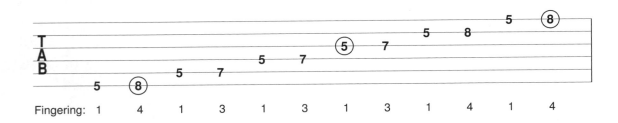

## 2nd Position C Major Pentatonic Scale

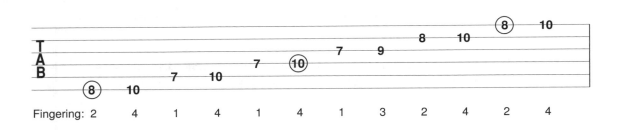

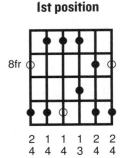

# 3rd Position C Major Pentatonic Scale

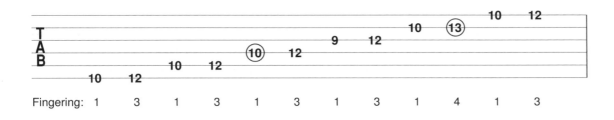

2nd position

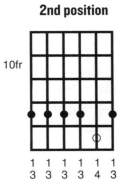

Fingering:  1   3   1   3   1   3   1   3   1   4   1   3

# 4th Position C Major Pentatonic Scale

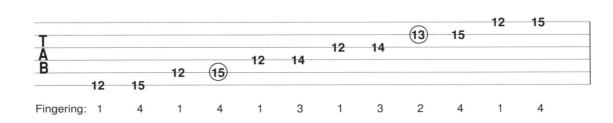

3rd position

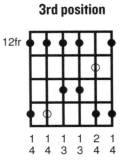

Fingering:  1   4   1   4   1   3   1   3   2   4   1   4

# 5th Position C Major Pentatonic Scale

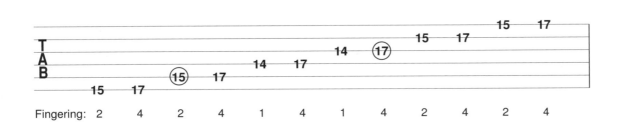

4th position

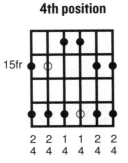

Fingering:  2   4   2   4   1   4   1   4   2   4   2   4

# Fast Blues in C (Sliding Rhythm)

This rhythm is a fast I - IV - V shuffle in C major. After learning this rhythm, you can solo along with the backing track using the C major pentatonic scales. The fingering is shown under the first staff; use the same fingering for the rest of the progression. When performing the slides and double-stops, lean your second finger downward slightly to deaden the string that's in between the two notes being played.

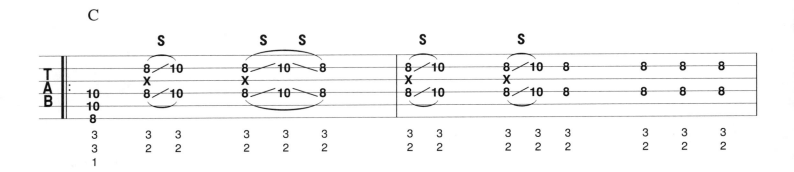

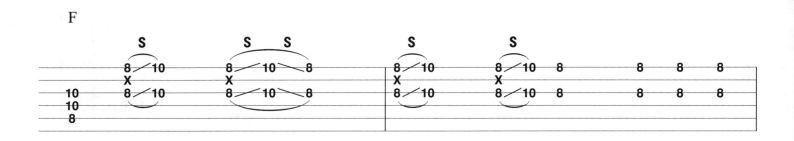

114

C

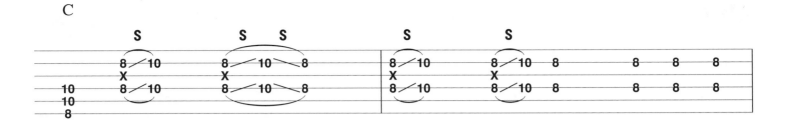

G                                                   F

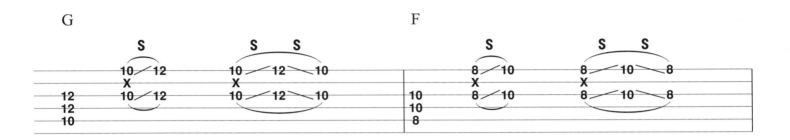

C

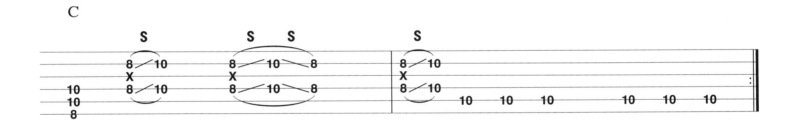

## Quick Tip!

### LEARN GRADUALLY AND HAVE REALISTIC GOALS

*Don't try to play a lot of things you aren't ready for. Be realistic about your capabilities as a beginner and learn gradually. If you progress at a steady, methodical rate, your technique and control of the guitar will become solid as you advance. Strive to master each new technique, chord or scale before moving on to something else. Attempting things that you're not quite ready for can discourage you instead of inspire you to play.*

# Combining Major and Minor Scales

You can create a call and response effect by switching back and forth between the major and minor keys while soloing. Compare the two scale positions below. Notice that the finger pattern is the same for both scales; the major starts at the 5th fret, the minor starts at the 8th fret. The difference is in the placement of the root notes. This forms an easy way for you to switch from major to minor just by moving the scale position three frets. To play a relative major pentatonic scale, you can move any of the minor pentatonic scale positions down three frets.

Try soloing over the Fast Blues in C from the previous section using both the major and minor pentatonics. You can solo for a few bars in major, then move three frets higher and solo in minor for a few bars to achieve a call and response effect.

## C Major Pentatonic Scale

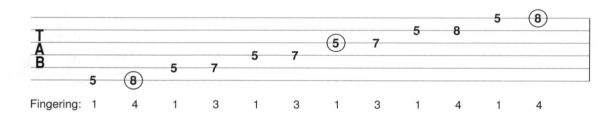

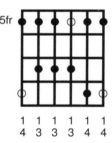

## C Minor Pentatonic Scale

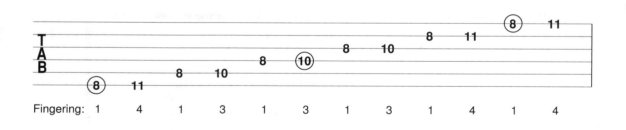

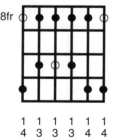

# Improvisation Exercise

Many blues solos are created around the expansion of a main riff or phrase. You can take a simple, recognizable melody and keep coming back to it or play slight variations of it. This main theme gives the listener something to grasp on to in the same way as a chorus or hook does.

The melody below is shown in three different octaves on the guitar. Play over the same C major backing track and try working out a solo around this simple melody. You can play it anywhere within the progression; these themes work especially well when used in a turnaround. This technique is also demonstrated in the video. Once you understand the concept, try creating your own themes and melodies to build leads around.

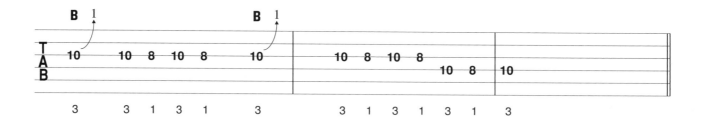

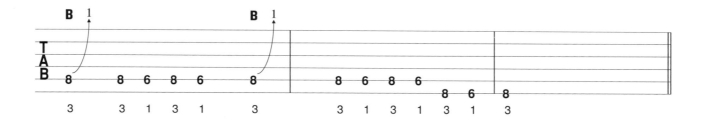

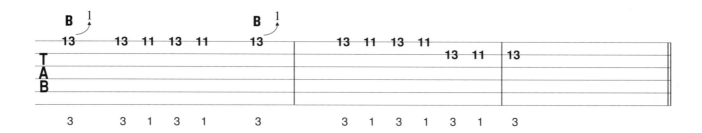

# Blues Rock Progression - Key of D

The following blues rock progression in D is played using a sixteenth note rhythm. The chord changes are based on a I - IV - V progression with the addition of a repeated, single note riff placed between the chords. Use alternate strumming and picking to get the steady, sixteenth notes up to speed. The chords are all barre chords and are shown as full barre chords in the tab staff. You'll notice that these chords are not always fully strummed on the DVD program. This is a good example of interpretation and the use of performance techniques to spice up a simple progression. By varying the accents, muting, or how much of the chord your pick actually strums, you can add character to the sound and style.

D                           N.C.

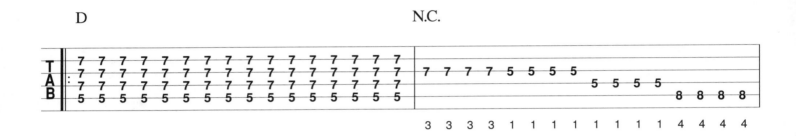

D

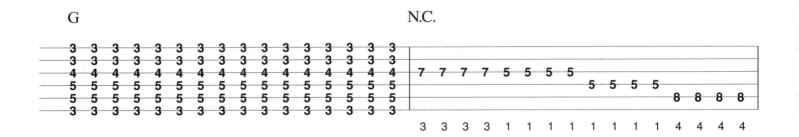

G                          N.C.

**D**

```
|-7--7--7--7--7--7--7--7--7--7--7--7--7--7--7--7-|-7--7--7--7--7--7--7--7--7--7--7--7--7--7--7--7-|
|-7--7--7--7--7--7--7--7--7--7--7--7--7--7--7--7-|-7--7--7--7--7--7--7--7--7--7--7--7--7--7--7--7-|
|-7--7--7--7--7--7--7--7--7--7--7--7--7--7--7--7-|-7--7--7--7--7--7--7--7--7--7--7--7--7--7--7--7-|
|-5--5--5--5--5--5--5--5--5--5--5--5--5--5--5--5-|-5--5--5--5--5--5--5--5--5--5--5--5--5--5--5--5-|
```

**A**                                                **N.C.**

```
|-5--5--5--5--5--5--5--5--5--5--5--5--5--5--5--5-|-------------------------------------------------|
|-5--5--5--5--5--5--5--5--5--5--5--5--5--5--5--5-|-------------------------------------------------|
|-6--6--6--6--6--6--6--6--6--6--6--6--6--6--6--6-|-7--7--7--7--5--5--5--5---------------------------|
|-7--7--7--7--7--7--7--7--7--7--7--7--7--7--7--7-|-------------------------5--5--5--5---------------|
|-7--7--7--7--7--7--7--7--7--7--7--7--7--7--7--7-|-------------------------------------8--8--8--8---|
|-5--5--5--5--5--5--5--5--5--5--5--5--5--5--5--5-|-------------------------------------------------|
```

```
                                                   3  3  3  3  1  1  1  1  1  1  1  1  4  4  4  4
```

**D**

```
|-7--7--7--7--7--7--7--7--7--7--7--7--7--7--7--7-|-7--7--7--7--7--7--7--7--7--7--7--7--7--7--7--7-||
|-7--7--7--7--7--7--7--7--7--7--7--7--7--7--7--7-|-7--7--7--7--7--7--7--7--7--7--7--7--7--7--7--7-||
|-7--7--7--7--7--7--7--7--7--7--7--7--7--7--7--7-|-7--7--7--7--7--7--7--7--7--7--7--7--7--7--7--7-||
|-5--5--5--5--5--5--5--5--5--5--5--5--5--5--5--5-|-5--5--5--5--5--5--5--5--5--5--5--5--5--5--5--5-||
```

After you have the rhythm pattern and speed mastered, you can try playing leads along with the backing track using the D minor pentatonic scales. Practice soloing with the sixteenth note lead pattern in different positions, and then create some of your own patterns. Fast sixteenth note rhythms aren't usually common in blues music, but they're used often in many rock styles. Blues techniques are often fused with other genres of music to create innovative new styles. Learning to play fast rhythms and leads in different musical styles is a great way to build coordination and strength in your picking hand, which will enable you to play clean and accurate leads at any tempo.

# Classic Old School Blues Turnarounds

Here's a standard, old school blues progression in E. This shuffle rhythm uses riffs, seventh chords and turnarounds. Follow the strumming patterns and fingering references that are indicated above and below the tab staff when necessary.

The turnarounds and endings are underneath the repeat brackets at the end of each repetition. A blues turnaround is a riff at the end of a progression designed to lead smoothly back to the beginning of the rhythm. Blues endings are similar to turnarounds, but are used to conclude songs with a unique flair. Both turnarounds incorporate standard riffs that lead into the V chord (dominant). The final ending uses an open string pull off and hammer on combination riff that leads into the I chord (tonic). The use of dominant seventh chords in the turnarounds and ending give it that classic blues sound.

Once you have the rhythm down, try soloing over the backing track using the E blues scales. This is a great blues rhythm to practice all of the soloing techniques you've learned throughout the program.

E

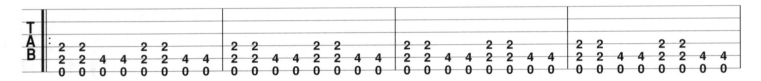

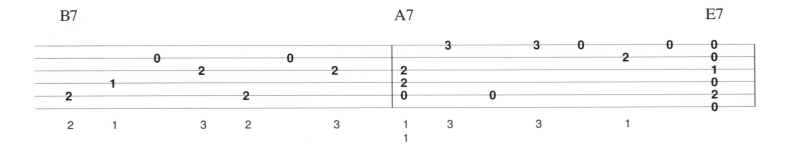

## Turnaround #1

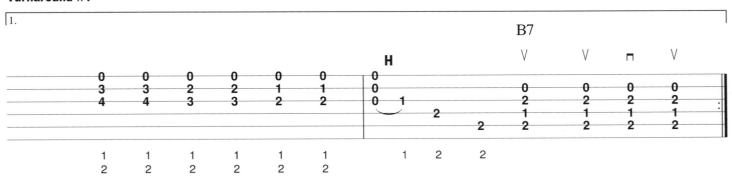

## Turnaround #2

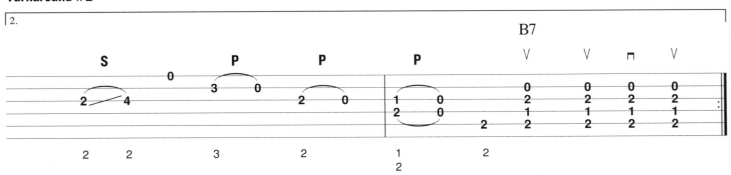

## Ending

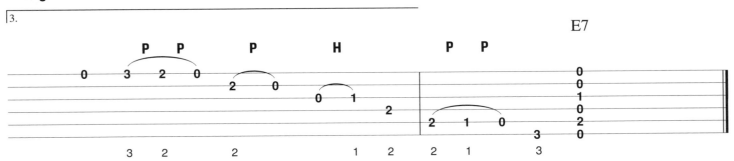

# Modern Blues Progression - Circle of Fourths

The following progression is a slow blues in the key of Am. The rhythm is counted in three's and each chord is arpeggiated (the notes of each chord are picked out separately). Finger and hold the chord in each measure and let its notes ring out together. Follow the finger numbers under the tab staff to show you the proper chord fingerings. Play along with the backing track and practice the rhythm's slow ballad feel. The chord change progresses in a pattern of fourths; the distance from one chord to the next is the interval of a fourth. This is a common change that is also used in many musical styles ranging from classical to metal.

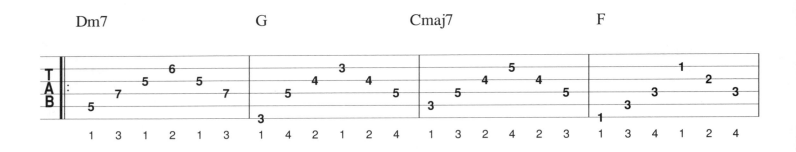

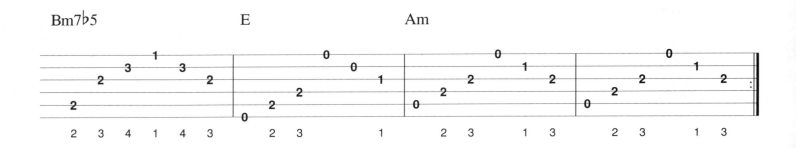

# Slide Technique and Rhythm

Slide guitar is a very popular technique used in blues. A slide is a cylinder worn on the ring finger of your fretting hand that allows you to slide notes and chords in a smooth, steady motion. Slides can be made of glass, metal, brass, or ceramic. You can even spontaneously use a shot glass or beer bottle as a slide.

In order to play pitches in tune with a slide, place the slide directly over the fret bar (not in between the frets). Use the frets as a visual reference point for where the notes will sound in tune. Touch the strings lightly with the slide; don't press down like you're fretting the note. Use the tip of the slide to play single notes or lay it flat to play chords. Open tunings work very well in conjunction with a slide because they allow you to slide full chords with one finger. Guitars that are set up to play with a slide usually have the action (string height) set a little higher than normal to keep the slide from hitting the frets.

A good way to begin to get the slide technique down is to play through the pentatonic scale using a slide. Try it in the 1st position, sliding from the first to the second notes along each string. Remember not to press down with the slide, just allow it to lightly touch the strings.

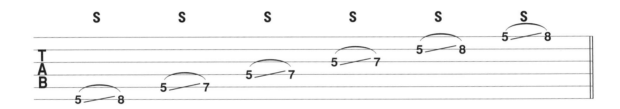

The following exercise is a typical blues-rock rhythm played with a slide. This riff has been used to make up countless songs, so it should sound very familiar to you. The first measure (before the repeat sign) is called a pickup. It represents a partial measure of music that leads into the main repeated riff.

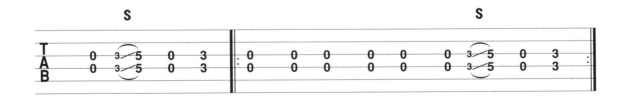

# E Blues Riff Rhythm

For the last section of this program, let's go over a single note riff rhythm in E. After you learn the rhythm, you can solo over the backing track using the E blues scales and all of the techniques we've covered. The progression is also based on a I - IV - V, 12-bar blues style; the chord names above the tab staff are there as a reference to outline the basic harmony.

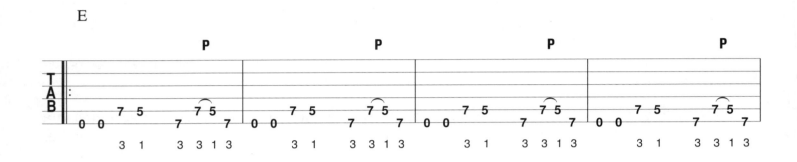

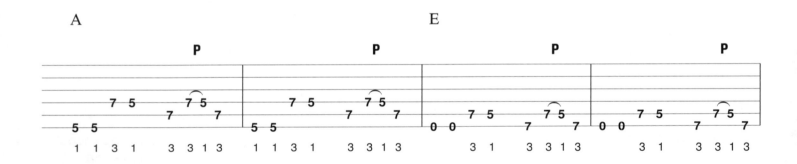

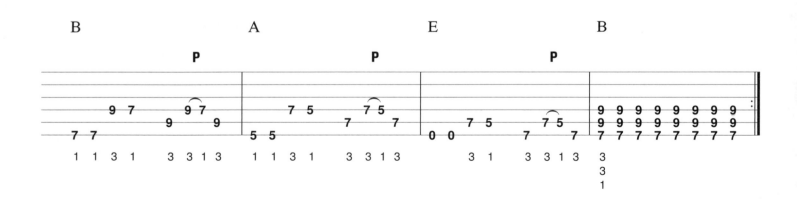

124

# E Blues Solo

The following solo is in the key of E. Try some of these riffs, then create your own and work on your improvisational skills using all of the techniques and styles you've learned. Log on to www.rockhousemethod.com and join our online community for additional information and resources.

E

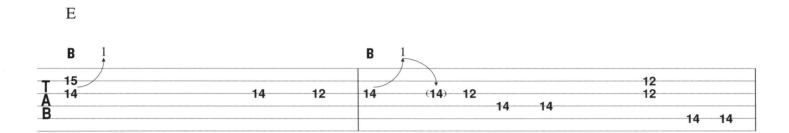

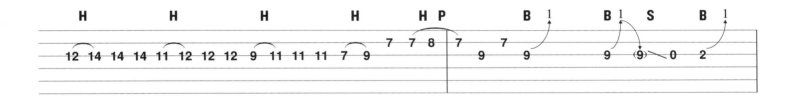

A

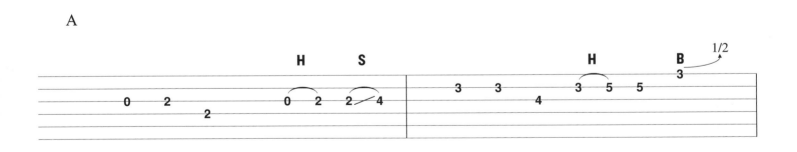

E

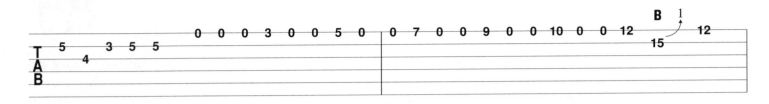

B

A

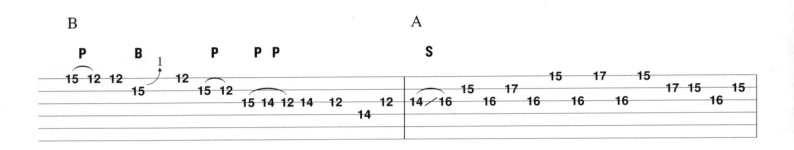

E

B

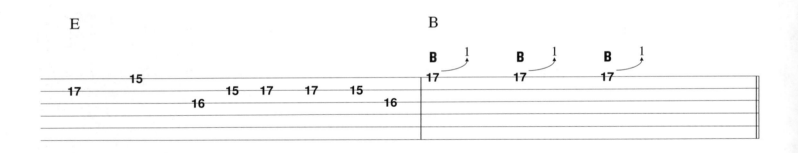

# C Major 3 Note Per String Scale Patterns

Are you ready to travel the neck of your guitar as free as the top shredders in the world? Here's a little secret amongst the pros: think linear. In this lesson we are going to cover three-notes per string patterns. All of the scale patterns we have learned up until now have been in a "box" type position. Now we are going to get every last inch of real estate on the fretboard. Get these seven patterns under your fingers to help you get the most out of your fretboard!

Before we begin to learn the six 3 note per string scale patterns, lets first look at how the C Major scale is laid out over the entire fretboard. From here you can compare how the 6 patterns work together like Legos® connecting to combine the entire span of the fretboard when aggregated.

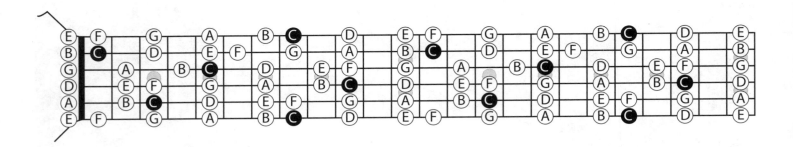

Now, here are the six patterns. Practice them daily with a metronome and gradually build up your speed playing them. Once you have them solidified under your fingers, try using techniques we have covered like hammer-ons and pull-offs to practice them with a legato feel. Also, try string skipping and Bi-dextral hammer-ons (tapping) to create new lead pattern sequences for your leads.

## Pattern I

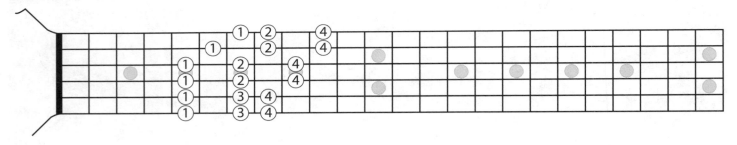

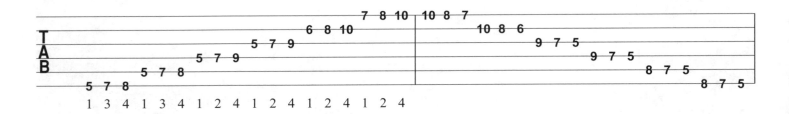

## Pattern 2

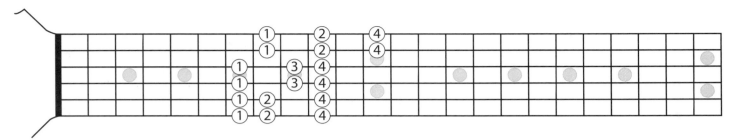

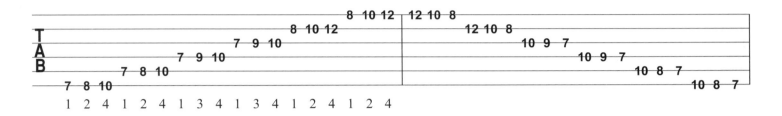

1 2 4 1 2 4 1 3 4 1 3 4 1 2 4 1 2 4

## Pattern 3

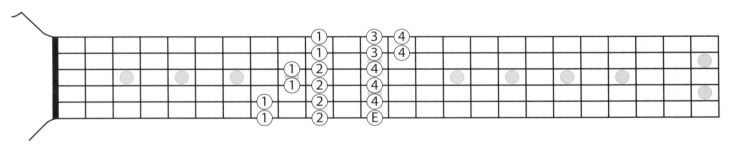

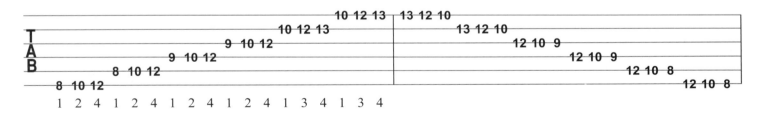

1 2 4 1 2 4 1 2 4 1 2 4 1 3 4 1 3 4

## Pattern 4

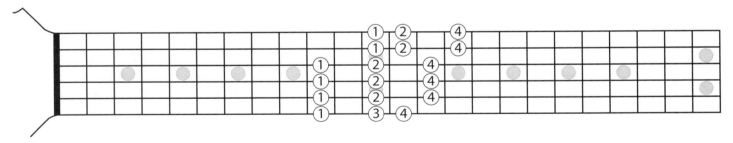

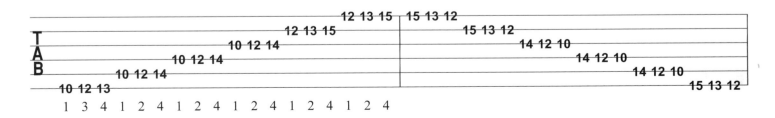

1 3 4 1 2 4 1 2 4 1 2 4 1 2 4 1 2 4

## Pattern 5

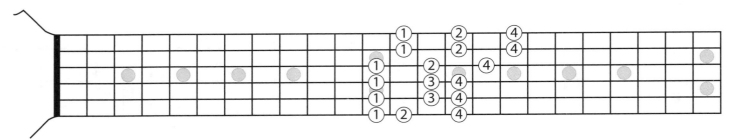

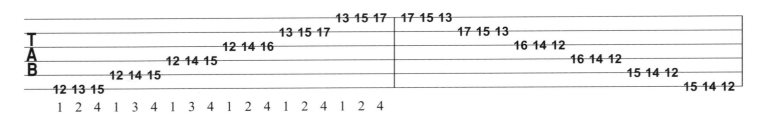

## Pattern 6

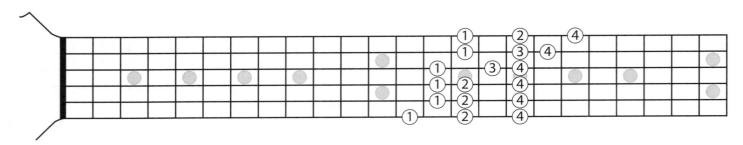

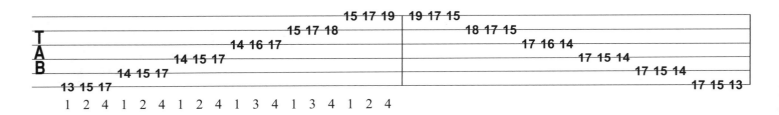

## Pattern 7

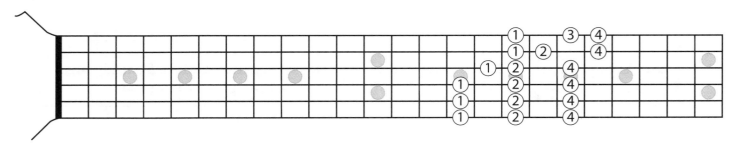

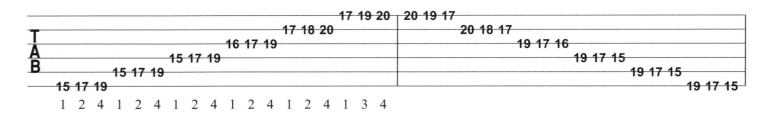

130

# Common Blues Progression Variations

The following examples are typical variations of the Blues progression. There are many variations that have been used throughout the decades. All of the following progressions are written in the key of "C." Transpose these progressions to all of the keys. Below each measure you will see the chord/key function to help you transpose these progressions easier. If you are unfamiliar with some of these chords, make sure you get a copy of "The Only Chord Book You Will Ever Need" from Rock House.

## Double "V" Turnaround 12 Bar

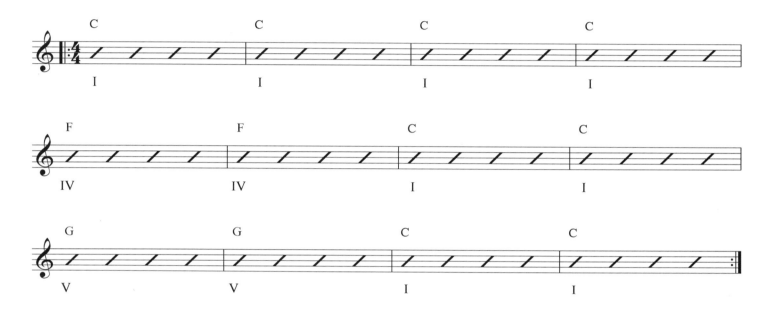

## Substituting THE "iv" Chord with a "I" Minor Chord

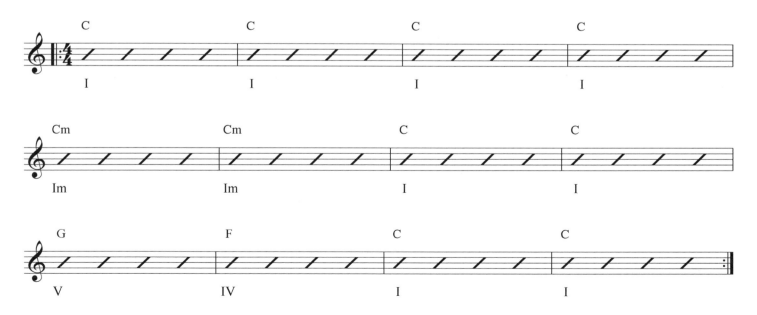

## Using a Dominant Chord Before Chord Changes

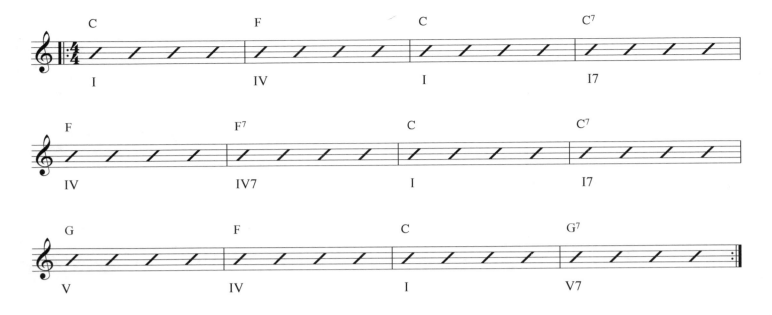

## 12 Bar Basie Blues Chord Progression

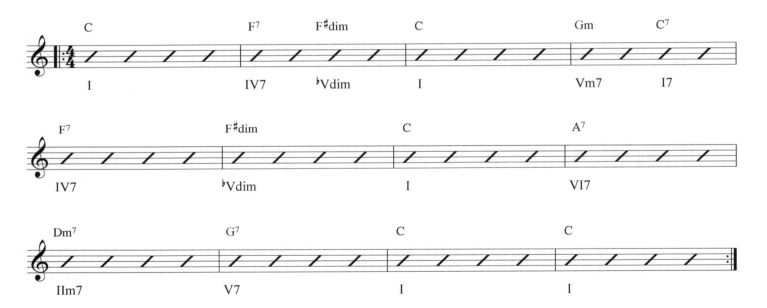

# Basic Jazz/Blues Progression

Notice the close similarities to the 12 Bar Basie Blues Progression you just learned.

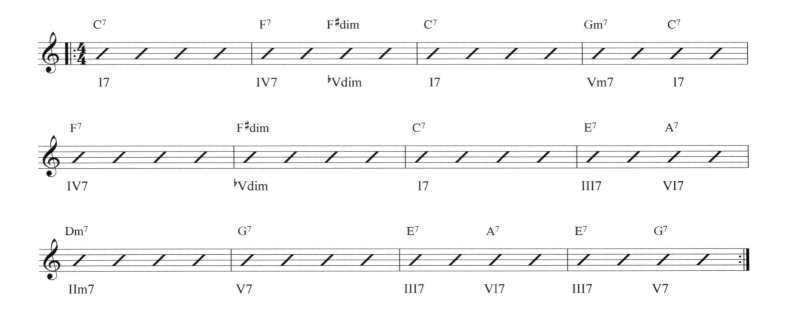

# 12 Bar Minor Blues Progression

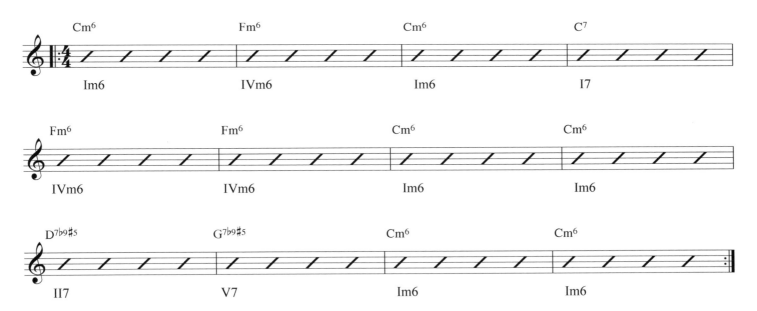

Some Blues progressions are more or less than 12 bars long. Here are a few examples of some different blues forms you may encounter on your journey to being a great Blues musician.

## 8 Bar Blues Progression

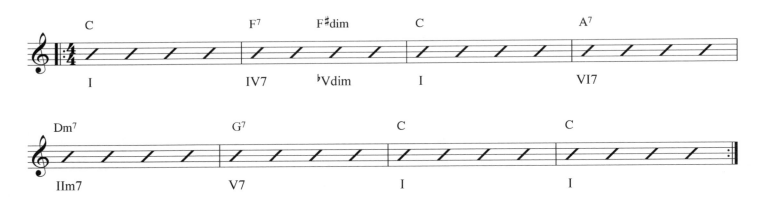

## 16 Bar Blues Progression

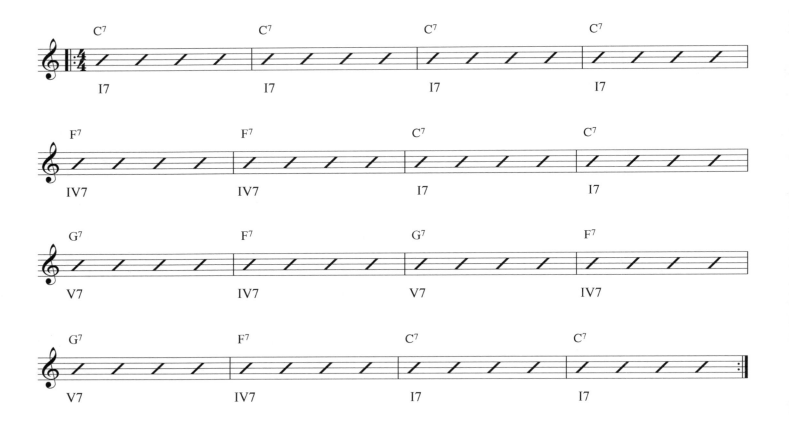

# Chord Glossary

Chords are the building blocks for songs. By learning new chords you expand your horizons for building song structures. You need to have chord knowledge to create your own masterpiece. I've compiled a group of chords that are great for music. They are all root C chords but many are movable and can be played in any key by moving them up or down the neck.

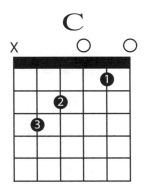  

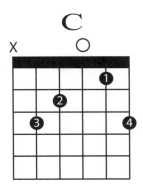  

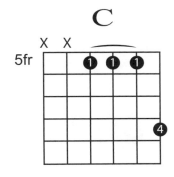  

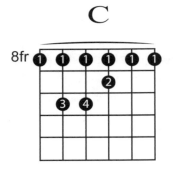

**C**

8fr

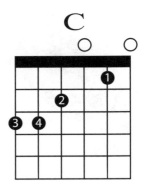

**C**

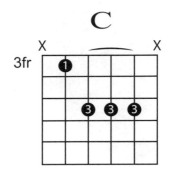

**C**

3fr

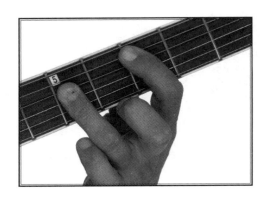

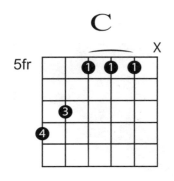

**C**

5fr

## C

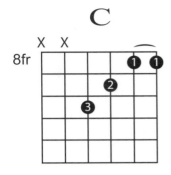

8fr

## Csus⁴

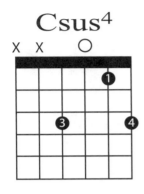

## Csus⁴

3fr

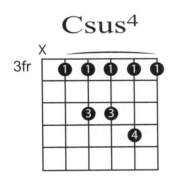

## Csus⁴

8fr

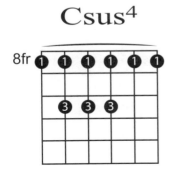

## Csus²

3fr

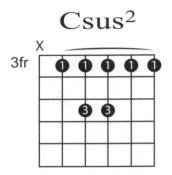

## Csus²

5fr

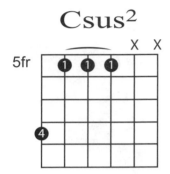

## Csus²

10fr

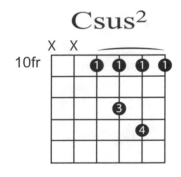

## C⁶

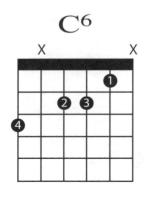

## C$^6$

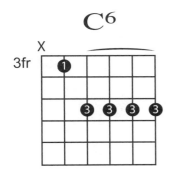

X
3fr ① ③ ③ ③ ③

## C$^6$

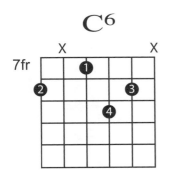

X    X
7fr ② ① ③ ④

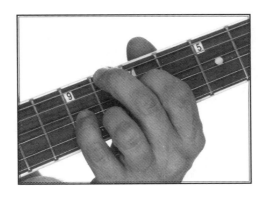

## C$^6$

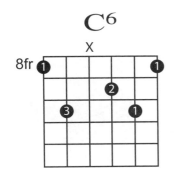

X
8fr ① ② ③ ① ①

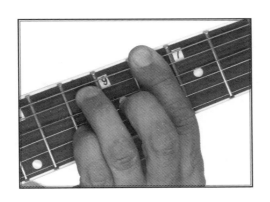

## Cmaj$^7$

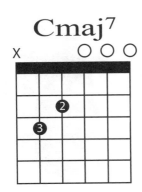

X    ○ ○ ○
② ③

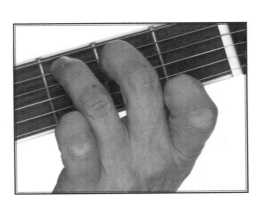

## Cmaj7

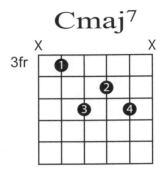

X                    X
3fr ① 
         ②
      ③    ④

## Cmaj7

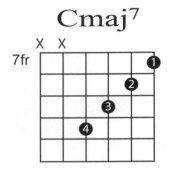

X  X
7fr                    ①
               ②
            ③
         ④

## Cmaj7

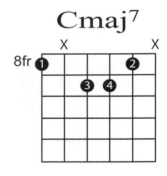

X                    X
8fr ①            ②
         ③    ④

## Cmaj9

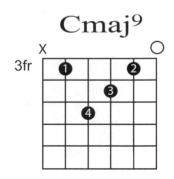

X                    ○
3fr ①            ②
               ③
         ④

140

## Cmaj⁹

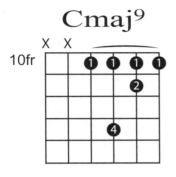

10fr

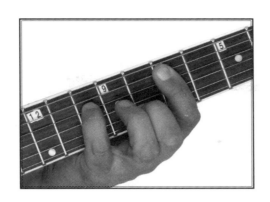

## Cmaj¹³

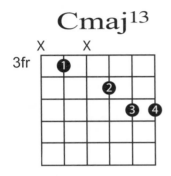

3fr

## Cmaj¹³

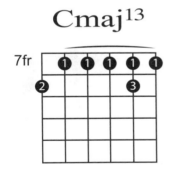

7fr

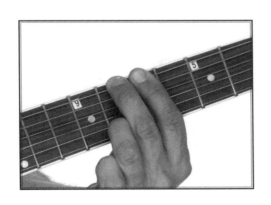

## Cm

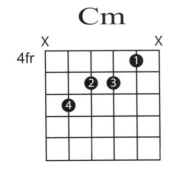

4fr

## Cm

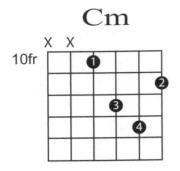

X X
10fr
① ②
③
④

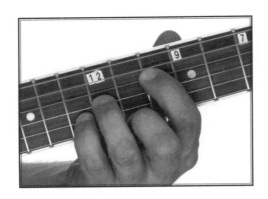

## Cm⁶

X ○ ○
① ②
④

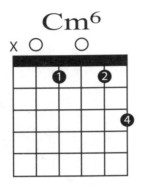

## Cm⁶

X X
①
② ③
④

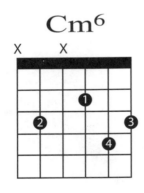

## Cm⁶

X X X
7fr
①
② ③ ③

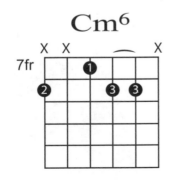

## Cm$^7$

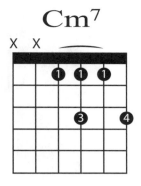

## Cm$^7$

3fr

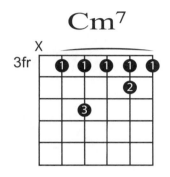

## Cm$^7$

8fr

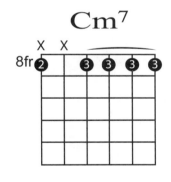

## Cm$^7$

10fr

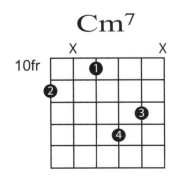

## Cm⁹

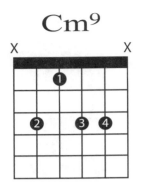

X       X

## Cm⁹

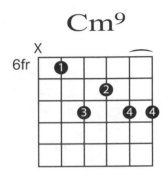

X

6fr

## Cm¹¹

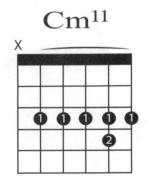

X

## Cm¹¹

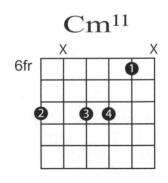

X       X

6fr

## Cm¹³

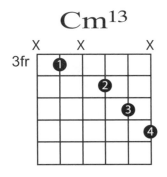

3fr

## Cm¹³

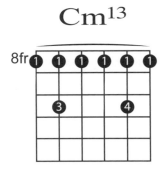

8fr

## Cm⁷♭⁵

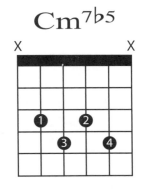

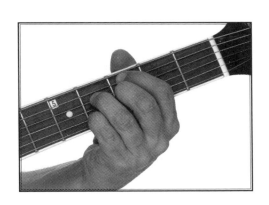

## Cm⁷♭⁵

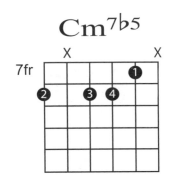

7fr

## Cm⁷♭5

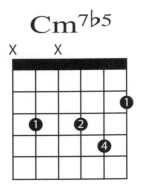

## Cm⁷♭5

10fr

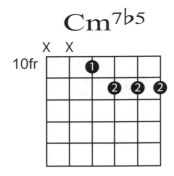

## Cm⁷♭5

8fr

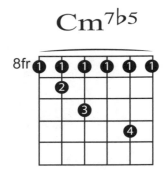

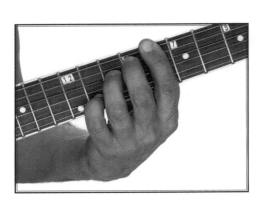

## C°7

5fr

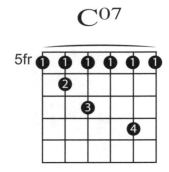

### C⁰7

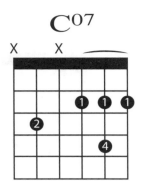

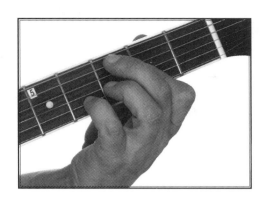

### C7

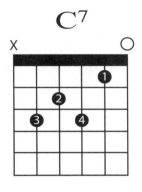

### C7

3fr

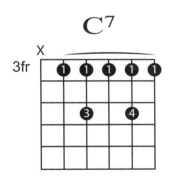

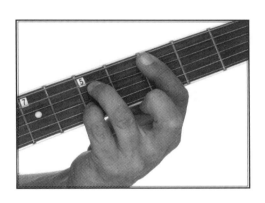

### C7

3fr

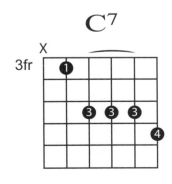

### C7

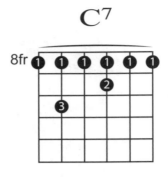

8fr

### C7

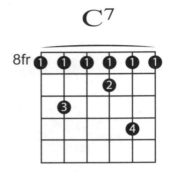

8fr

### C7

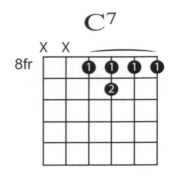

8fr    X    X

### C7sus4

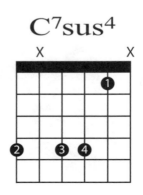

X    X

## C⁷sus⁴

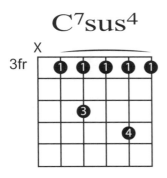

X
3fr
①①①①①
③
④

## C7♭5

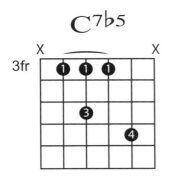

X        X
3fr
①①①
③
④

## C7♭5

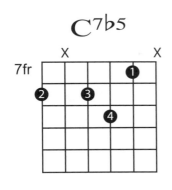

X        X
7fr
①
②  ③
④

## C⁹

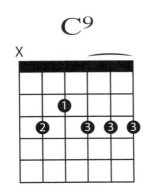

X
①
②  ③ ③ ③

## C⁹

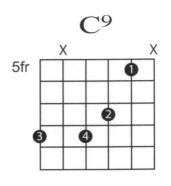

X      X
5fr

## C⁹

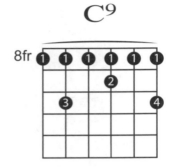

8fr

## C⁹sus⁴

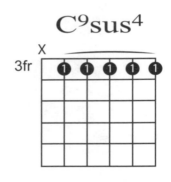

X
3fr

## C⁹sus⁴

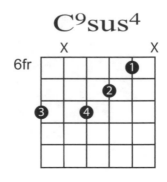

X      X
6fr

150

## C¹³

X          X

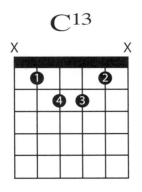

## C¹³

5fr

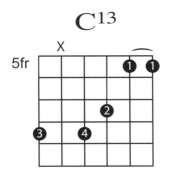

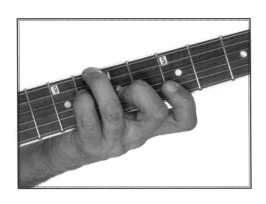

## C¹³

X   X

8fr

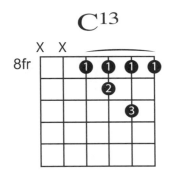

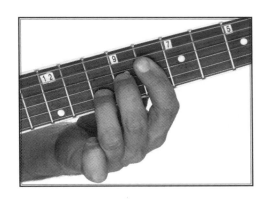

## C¹³

X          X

8fr

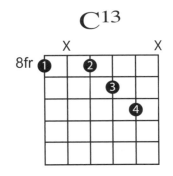

151

## C+

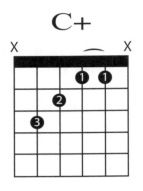

X                    X

## C+

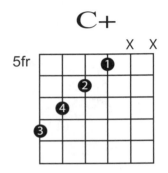

X  X

5fr

## C5

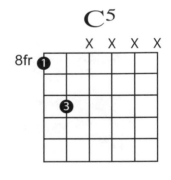

X  X  X  X

8fr

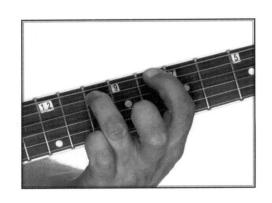

## C5

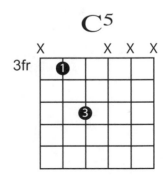

X      X  X  X

3fr

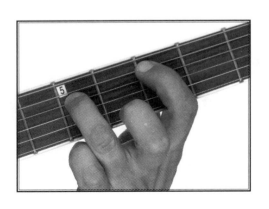

# Finding the Relative Minor Scale

Every major key has a minor scale that shares the same key signature. The minor scale that shares the same key signature is called the relative minor scale or key. The relative minor scale begins and ends on the 6th degree of the major scale. Count up to the 6th degree of any major scale, this note will be the root note of the relative minor scale. Now from the 6th degree play the notes of the major scale up one octave to the next 6th degree of the scale. Let's look at this in the key of C major that you learned earlier.

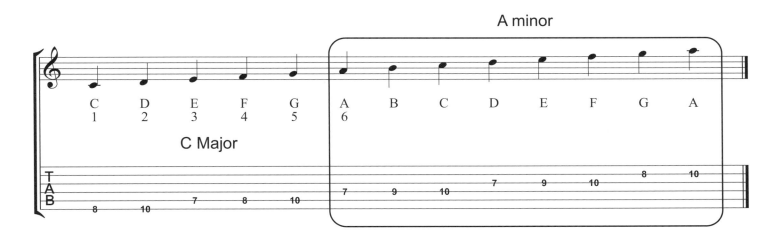

Here is the same process in tab for the C major and G major keys.

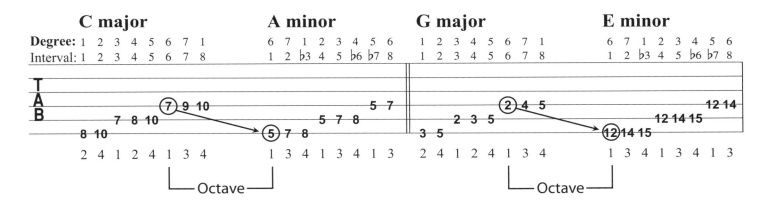

Now you are probably wondering why the importance of the minor scale. It is still the same notes of the major scale, right? So what's the difference? Even though they are the same notes the overall feel of the scale is different. This is because the order of the whole-steps and half-steps is different. The major scale if you recall is W-W-H-W-W-W-H. The minor scale is W-H-W-W-H-W-W. The changed order of the whole and half-steps gives the minor scale a sad or melancholy type of sound whereas the major scale has a powerful and bright sound to it. Also keep in mind that the term "relative" is a loose one. The minor scale functions independently as its own entity, just as your cousin does. You are relative to each other; however, you both make your own ways through the world. You and your cousin still come together as a family just as the two scales sometimes come together within one song.

# All Keys Relative Minor

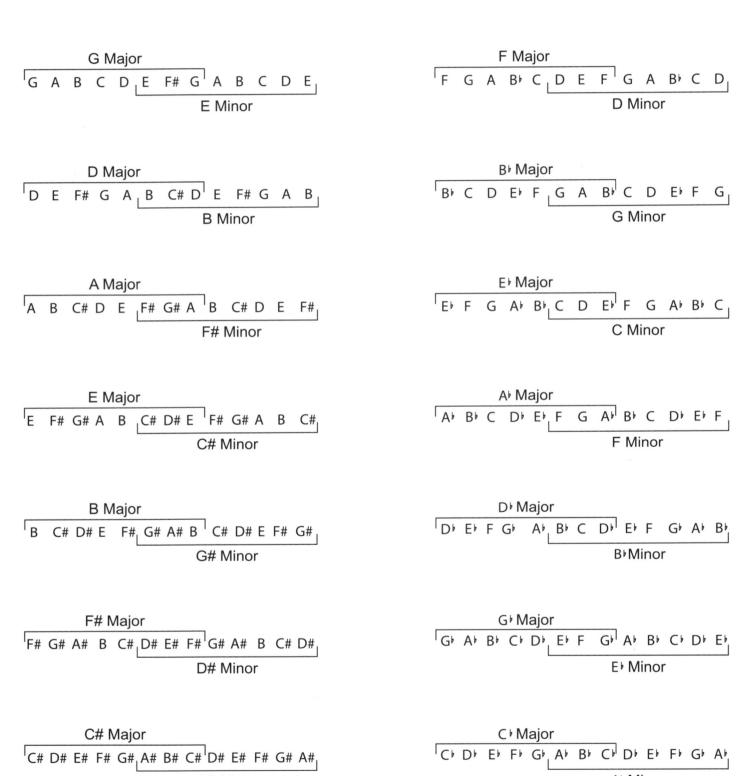

# Full Major Scales

## A Major

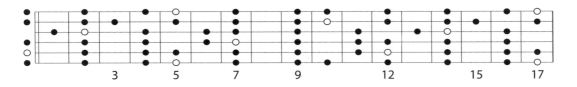

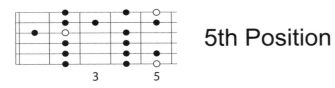

5th Position

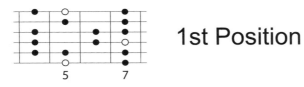

1st Position

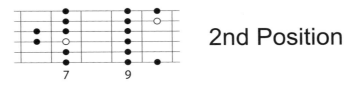

2nd Position

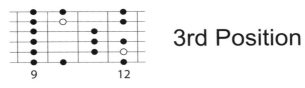

3rd Position

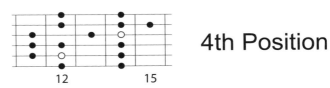

4th Position

# Three Note Per String Minor Scales

## A Minor

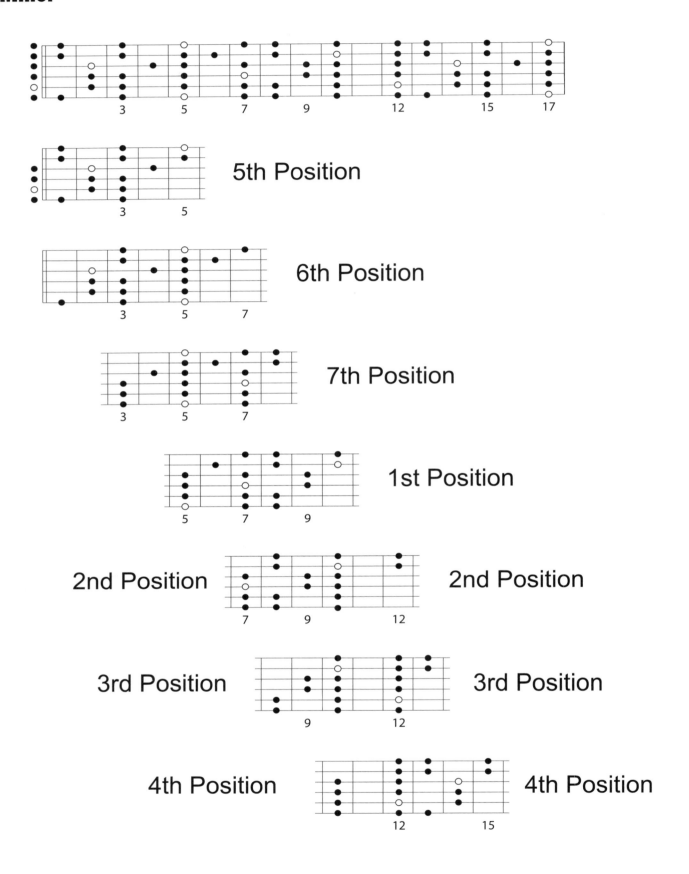

5th Position

6th Position

7th Position

1st Position

2nd Position      2nd Position

3rd Position      3rd Position

4th Position      4th Position

# Major Pentatonic Scales

## A Major

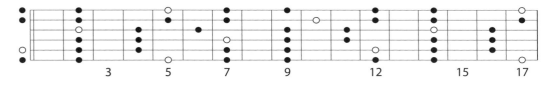

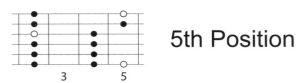 5th Position

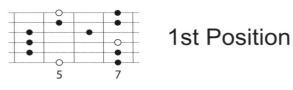 1st Position

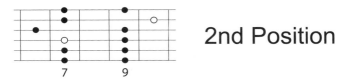 2nd Position

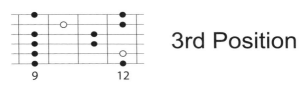 3rd Position

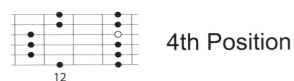 4th Position

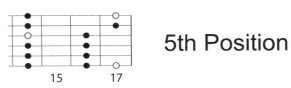 5th Position

# Minor Pentatonic Scales

## A Minor

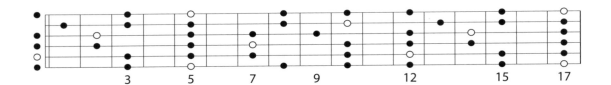

4th Position

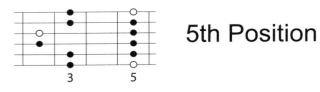

5th Position

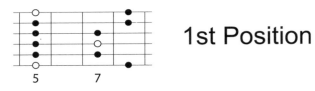

1st Position

2nd Position

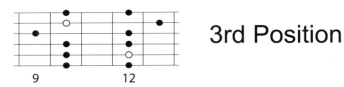

3rd Position

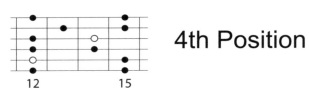

4th Position

# Changing Your Strings

Old guitar strings may break or lose their tone and become harder to keep in tune. You might feel comfortable at first having a teacher or someone at a music store change your strings for you, but eventually you will need to know how to do it yourself. Changing the strings on a guitar is not as difficult as it may seem and the best way to learn how to do this is by practicing. Guitar strings are fairly inexpensive and you may have to go through a few to get it right the first time you try to restring your guitar. How often you change your strings depends entirely on how much you play your guitar, but if the same strings have been on it for months, it's probably time for a new set.

Most strings attach at the headstock in the same way, however electric and acoustic guitars vary in the way in which the string is attached at the bridge. Before removing the old string from the guitar, examine the way it is attached to the guitar and try to duplicate that with the new string. Acoustic guitars may use removable bridge pins that fasten the end of the string to the guitar by pushing it into the bridge and securing it there. On some electric guitars, the string may need to be threaded through a hole in the back of the body

Follow the series of photos below for a basic description of how to change a string. Before trying it yourself, read through the quick tips for beginners on the following page.

Use a string winder to loosen the string.

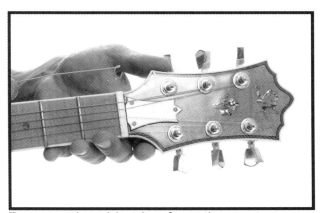
Remove the old string from the post.

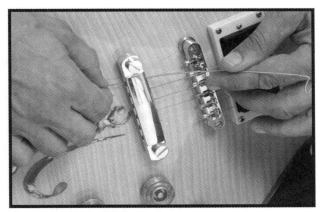
Pull the string through the bridge and discard it.

Remove the new string from the packaging and uncoil it.

Thread the end of the new string through the bridge.

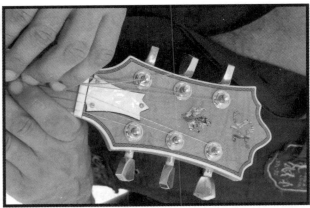

Pull the string along the neck and thread it through the small hole on the tuning post.

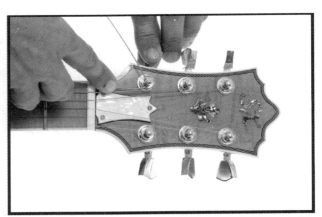

Hold the string in place just after the nut with your finger and tighten up the slack in the string with the machine head.

Carefully tighten the string and tune it to the proper pitch.

You can cut the old string off the guitar but you may want to unwind it instead and save it as a spare in case you break a string later.

Check to make sure you have the correct string in your hand before putting it on the guitar. The strings may be color coded at the end to help you identify them.

Be sure to wind the string around the tuning post in the proper direction (see photos), and leave enough slack to wind the string around the post several times. The string should wind around the post underneath itself to form a nice, neat coil.

Once the extra slack is taken up and the string is taught, tune it very gradually to pitch, being careful not to overtighten and accidentally break the new string.

Once the string is on the guitar and tightened up, you can cut the excess string sticking out from the tuning post with a wire cutter. The sharp tail end that is left can be bent downward with the wire cutter to get it out of the way and avoid cutting or stabbing your finger on it.

Check the ends of the string to make sure it is sitting correctly on the proper saddle and space on the nut.

New strings will go out of tune very quickly until they are broken in. You can gently massage the new string with your thumbs and fingers once it's on the guitar, slightly stretching the string out and helping to break it in. Then retune the string and repeat this process a few times for each string.

# Guitar Accessories

## Strings & Picks

Strings and picks are both available in different gauges. Heavier gauge strings produce a thicker, fuller sound; lighter gauges are thinner, easier to bend, and great for soloing. There are many different types of picks in different thicknesses. A heavy pick may offer you more control for lead playing, but medium and light picks have a flexibility that's good for rhythm playing. A fingerpick is a type of ring that you wear on your thumb for downpicking, allowing all of your fingers to be available for more complex fingerpicking. When changing your strings, you'll probably want to use a string winder. A string winder is a simple gadget that fits right over the machine heads so that you can quickly wind or unwind a string.

String winder

## Music Stands & Metronomes

As soon as you begin your first guitar lesson, you'll notice how important it is to have a music stand. Whenever you try to learn a new song from sheet music, or even go through a lesson in this book, you'll want to have the music right in front of you where it's close and easy to read. Don't try to balance a book on your lap or read it from the floor. If you're practicing scales and exercises or working out a difficult new guitar line, you can use a metronome to set a steady practice tempo and keep yourself in time. There are mechanical or electronic models, or you can download the free one from www.rockhousemethod.com and use your computer to keep time.

Electronic pocket metronome

## Capos & Slides

A capo is a moveable clamp that attaches to the neck of the guitar and barres across all six strings. Whichever fret the capo is placed at can then be thought of as the nut; the capo transposes the entire guitar to that position, making it possible to play all of the open chords there. Many acoustic players prefer the full open chord sound and use capos almost exclusively. Capos are popular at the 1st, 2nd, 3rd, 5th and 7th frets, but you can place a capo anywhere at all on the neck. A capo at the 12th fret transposes the guitar one octave higher and gives it a bright, mandolin tone.

A capo is clamped to the neck.

Capo properly placed at the 2nd fret.

An essential element of the blues guitar sound is the slide. A slide is a sleeve (usually glass) that fits over the ring finger of your left hand. With a slide you can slide notes or chords in a steady, smooth motion, making the guitar "talk." Slide guitar is also very popular in many rock styles, and can be heard in songs like "Freebird" and "Bad to the Bone."

A slide can be worn on your ring finger.

## Pickups & Effects

If your acoustic guitar is an electric-acoustic, it already has a pickup in it. If not, you can get a separate pickup that attaches to the guitar's sound hole. In basic terms, a pickup is like the guitar's microphone; the vibrations from the strings are magnetically picked up and turned into a signal that you can plug into an amp or PA system. An acoustic guitar doesn't need to be plugged in for you to hear it, but once it is, you can add effects like reverb, chorus, even distortion. With newer USB converters and software, you can also plug your guitar into a computer and play your way through cyberspace. Just connect right to your pc and you can get access to a whole arsenal of software featuring guitar effects, amp sounds, interactive lessons and virtual recording studios.

# Tuners

An electronic tuner is a necessity for any gigging guitarist, and tuners have become so common that they're often included in other effects units. Tuners are also sometimes put right into a guitar's electronics. If you don't have a tuner, you can download the free online tuner at our support website.

# Straps

Acoustic guitar straps can attach at the body if there's a strap button there. If not, a strap can be tied to the headstock between the nut and the machine heads. Straps come in a variety of materials and styles. When picking out a strap, try to find one that's both comfortable and that looks good with your guitar. Also available are strap locks (locking buttons that will keep the strap secured to the guitar).

# Cords

Investing a few dollars more to get a nice, heavy duty guitar cord is worthwhile. The cheaper ones don't last very long, while a professional quality cable can work perfectly for years. Some of the better cords even include a lifetime warranty. Cords also come in a variety of lengths, gauges and colors.

# Cases & Stands

The two main types of guitar cases are hardshell cases and softshell cases. Hardshell cases are more expensive and have a sturdy construction designed for maximum protection during travel. A much lighter and smaller alternative to the traditional guitar case is a gig bag: a padded, zippered guitar glove that is carried over the shoulders like a backpack. Guitar stands are usually collapsible and easy to take with you, but you can also use one at home to keep your guitar on display when you're not practicing.

# Make Your Own Tool Kit

Put together your own tool kit by keeping all of the important tools and spare parts you need in one place, like a small backpack or a compartment inside your guitar case. You should always have spare strings, a string winder, picks, batteries, and any small screwdrivers or wrenches that fit your guitar. You can purchase a multipurpose tool designed especially for guitarists (sort of like a pocket knife without the knife) that contains a few different types of screwdrivers and an assortment of allen wrenches. Some other good things to keep with you: wire cutters, fuses if your amp uses them, guitar polish and a soft cloth, music paper and pencil, and duct tape. You may also want to keep a small recording device handy to record your own musical ideas and use them to start writing your own songs.

# Practice Tips

To ensure constant progress and high motivation you have to develop practice habits that will keep you interested and challenged. Great practice habits will result in better overall playing and take you to the next level. As you move forward with your practice routine there are a few things you should do:

1. Practice consistently, I have had many students come to me and say I missed four days of practice and on the fifth day I played 4 hours. This is not the way to practice and see results because you do not give your fingers a chance to gain muscle memory. Practice every day even if it is for a short amount of time, be consistent.

2. Have a practice spot set up so you can have privacy to focus on your playing. It is a great idea to have a music stand to help position your music so you can sit comfortably. I remember when I started playing and I would lay my music on my bed and twist my neck to try to read and hold my guitar up properly, it was a real pain in the neck!

3. Always have your guitar out of the case, I use the expression "out of sight out of mind" if you see your guitar sitting there on a stand you are more prone to pick it up and play. When it's in a case under your bed its work to take it out and this may detour you from practicing. Besides when your friends come over your house and see your guitar they will be impressed!

4. Set a scheduled practice time each day, say you want to practice before school or work every day make this time a routine then later in the day you can play for fun and jam a little more.

# Creating a Practice Routine

As you evolve as a guitarist you will be constantly changing your practice outline. You should combine a series of components in your practice routine that will help you develop all aspects of your playing. Here is a list of my favorites.

## 1. Technique exercises for the left hand –
This is an exercise that challenges the coordination of your fretting hand. Many hammer on and pull off exercises work well to develop your fretting hand. These are usually repetitive exercises. Build speed gradually and practice them with a metronome

## 2. Technique exercises for developing your picking -
This is an exercise that challenges the coordination of your pick hand. Multiple string repetitive sequences are great pick exercises. You should build speed gradually and practice these with a metronome

## 3. Scales and patterns –
Use seven note and pentatonic scales in all different keys. Practice them with patterns of 2's, 3's and 4's always using alternate picking. Mix it up week by week to challenge your fingers.

## 4. Performance pieces –
This would be a song that you wish to learn that you haven't started yet. Pick a song that you want to learn have it on CD or tab and start picking it apart…literally!

## 5. Creating leads over progressions (backing tracks) -

This is where you get creative and jam a little to make melodies and leads. You can use jam backing tracks that have progressions of bass, drums and rhythm. Another way to do this is to pick your favorite CD and jam along pretending that you are a member of the band. Mimic the lead singer's melodies and play riffs and phrasings along with the track. This is a great way to learn to play melodically.

## 6. Classical pieces –

I like to use single string classical pieces here like Mozart Sonata #11 or #16 , they are almost always very challenging and they sound cool with a bit of distortion kicked in too.

## 7. Fun playing –

This is where you play things you know already, crank the amp up and rip into some guitar and have some fun!

## 8. Mental perception (visualization away from your instrument) –

Even though you may not be able to have your guitar with you all day long every day that doesn't mean you can't practice. Visualization is so important. Just going through your scales and the notes on the neck in your mind paints a visual picture that will help you to fly across the strings with ease. When you can see it in your mind your fingers will follow.

# Practice Log

Here is a chart you can copy to keep track of your practice routine as well as your progress. The example line shows that all week you practice the E blues scales and log your final metronome speed.

| Task | Day 1 | Day 2 | Day 3 | Day 4 | Day 5 | Day 6 | Day 7 |
|---|---|---|---|---|---|---|---|
| E BLUES SCALES w/ METRONOME | ✓ 60BPM | ✓ 60BPM | ✓ 65BPM | ✓ 70BPM | ✓ 85BPM | ✓ 90BPM | ✓ 95BPM |
| | | | | | | | |
| | | | | | | | |
| | | | | | | | |
| | | | | | | | |
| | | | | | | | |
| | | | | | | | |
| | | | | | | | |
| | | | | | | | |
| | | | | | | | |
| | | | | | | | |

# Crossword

Find the famous guitarists that played the songs listed below
**Answers on page 170**

**Across**

1. WELCOME TO THE JUNGLE
6. LUCILLE
8. I LOVE ROCK AND ROLL
9. PURPLE HAZE
10. MORE THAN A FEELING
11. IRON MAN
15. ERUPTION
16. KILLING IN THE NAME OF
18. SATISFACTION
19. CAT SCRATCH FEVER
20. REBEL YELL
23. WALK THIS WAY
25. PEACE SELLS
26. FRANKENSTEIN
31. SURRENDER
32. CROSSFIRE
33. MY GENERATION
34. SMOKE ON THE WATER
35. STAIRWAY TO HEAVEN

**Down**

2. ENTER SANDMAN
3. SURFING WITH THE ALIEN
4. SMELLS LIKE TEEN SPIRIT
5. DETROIT ROCK CITY
7. LIGHT MY FIRE
10. LIVIN' ON A PRAYER
12. MAGIC MAN
13. SUGAR MAGNOLIA
14. TAXMAN
17. PURPLE RAIN
21. BLACK MAGIC WOMAN
22. GO YOUR OWN WAY
24. HIGHWAY TO HELL
27. CRAZY TRAIN
28. TUSH
29. LAYLA
30. KISS ME DEADLY
34. JOHNNY B. GOODE

# Word Search

Find the 14 parts of the acoustic guitar listed in Chapter 1
**Answers on page 170**

```
X  T  A  E  Q  Q  D  P  N  H  J  S  Q  A  W  K  K  Y  A  I
V  B  V  H  L  Y  I  I  P  P  T  X  V  F  F  U  F  F  J  V
R  R  B  E  C  O  M  C  Z  O  G  S  W  I  Z  O  F  J  Q  E
Y  I  U  A  D  H  O  K  N  S  Q  N  W  Z  B  G  T  J  T  Z
Q  D  D  D  D  Y  V  G  G  I  D  B  P  F  S  U  W  S  Y  N
N  G  E  S  E  R  O  U  O  T  X  Z  N  X  T  Y  W  O  B  V
Z  E  Q  T  Z  D  O  A  X  I  H  G  U  V  R  C  G  U  R  V
B  P  B  O  T  H  F  R  M  O  M  V  T  S  A  B  B  N  I  F
L  I  R  C  G  H  G  D  G  N  A  N  Z  L  P  F  X  D  D  V
L  N  Q  K  C  N  E  C  K  M  C  Y  U  K  B  C  Z  H  G  A
K  S  B  K  C  P  G  K  S  A  H  P  N  R  U  S  N  O  E  V
W  A  O  O  S  D  N  H  T  R  I  O  D  H  T  W  D  L  V  H
J  D  B  F  N  B  C  X  I  K  N  X  M  V  T  O  Q  E  M  Q
X  D  X  Y  R  C  K  I  M  E  E  J  S  V  O  Q  Z  A  U  W
X  L  M  Z  Q  E  W  I  T  R  H  C  D  N  N  U  I  U  X  N
M  E  K  T  C  M  T  H  N  S  E  J  M  W  O  D  P  C  N  D
Z  Q  Q  X  B  X  C  S  T  Q  A  W  Q  E  Z  W  N  O  G  N
F  R  E  T  B  O  A  R  D  B  D  U  Y  M  Q  F  X  U  G  C
T  R  B  A  Q  R  D  U  M  G  S  R  W  A  S  U  D  Z  Q  L
R  X  X  S  N  F  Z  Y  F  R  J  H  B  A  F  W  P  Q  U  W
```

# JOHNNY BLUES

Here's the first part of the inspirational piece "Johnny Blues" from my CD, **Drive**. This is a perfect example of how some of the best melodies can be suprisingly easy to play. The audio for this section is available on the included CD. You can also download this track as well as other songs from **Drive** at www.rockhousemethod.com.

*- John McCarthy*

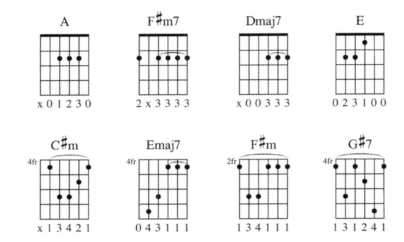

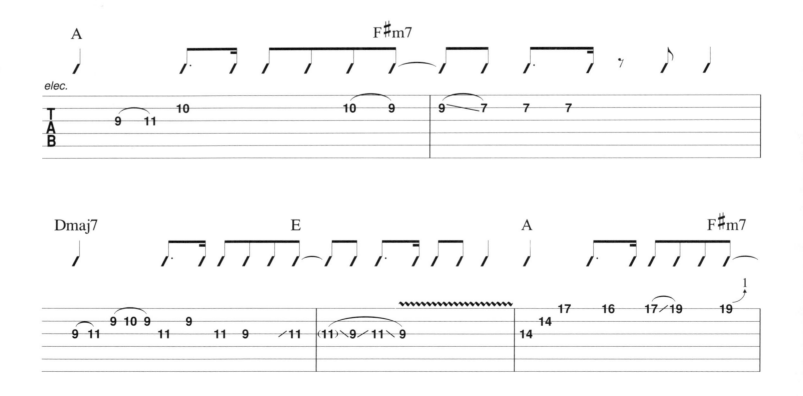

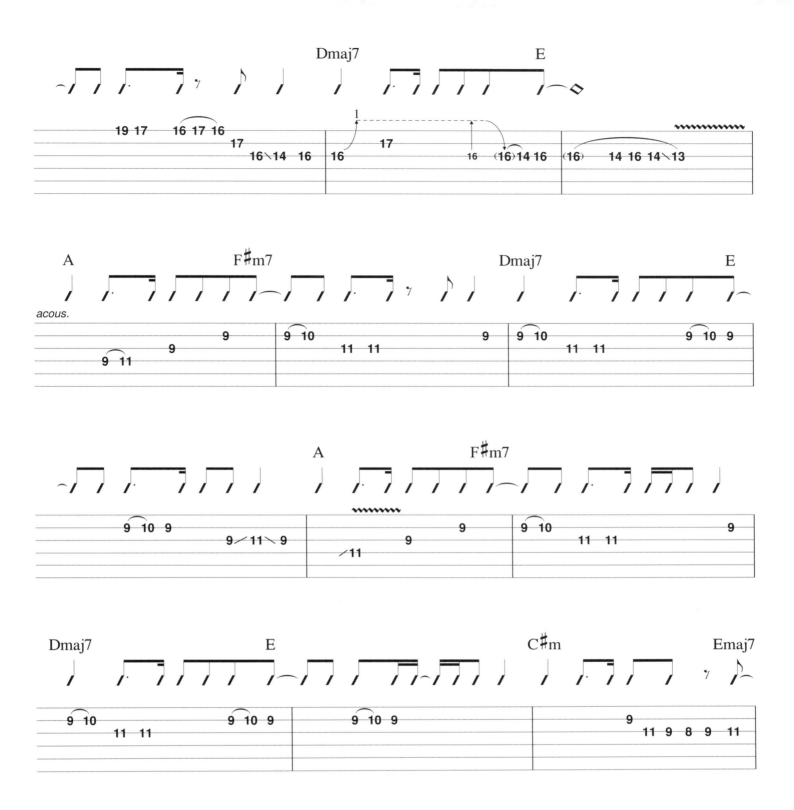
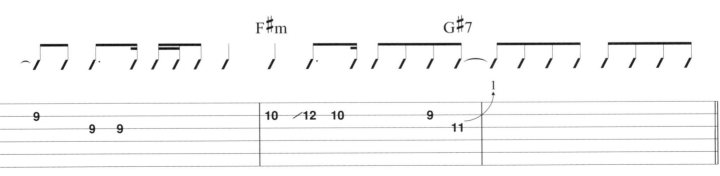

# Crossword and Word Search Answer Keys

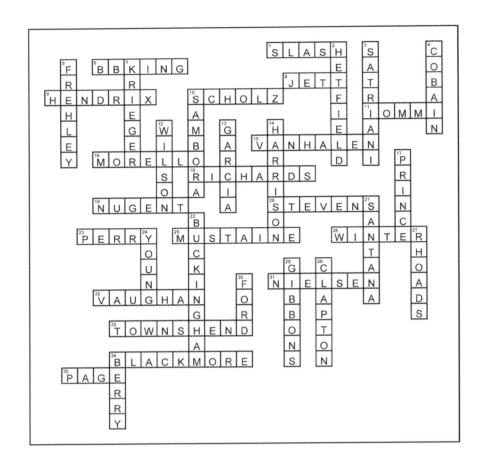

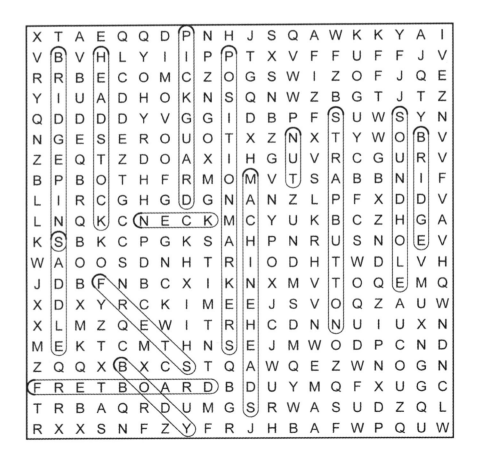

TAB

TAB

TAB

TAB

TAB

TAB

TAB

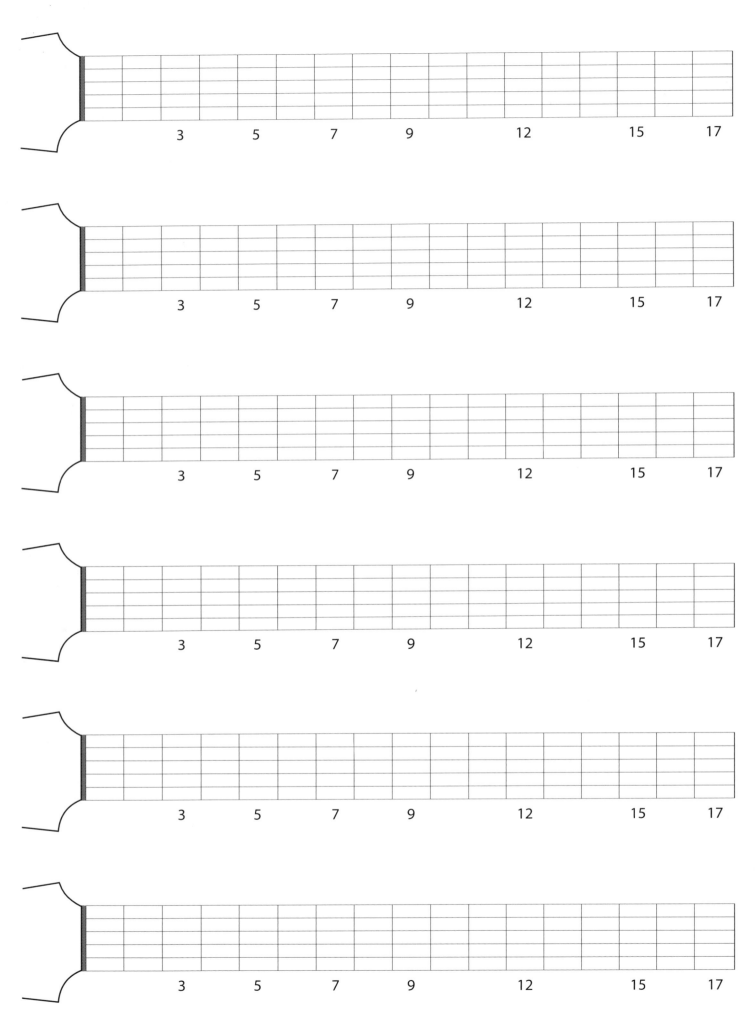

# About the Author

## John McCarthy
## Creator of
## The Rock House Method

John is the creator of The Rock House Method®, the world's leading musical instruction system. Over his 30 plus year career, he has written, produced and/or appeared in more than 100 instructional products. Millions of people around the world have learned to play music using John's easy-to-follow, accelerated programs.

John is a virtuoso musician who has worked with some of the industry's most legendary entertainers. He has the ability to break down, teach and communicate music in a manner that motivates and inspires others to achieve their dreams of playing an instrument.

As a musician and songwriter, John blends together a unique style of rock, metal, funk and blues in a collage of melodic compositions. Throughout his career, John has recorded and performed with renowned musicians including Doug Wimbish (Joe Satriani, Living Colour, The Rolling Stones, Madonna, Annie Lennox), Grammy Winner Leo Nocentelli, Rock & Roll Hall of Fame inductees Bernie Worrell and Jerome "Big Foot" Brailey, Freekbass, Gary Hoey, Bobby Kimball, David Ellefson (founding member of seven time Grammy nominee Megadeth), Will Calhoun (B.B. King, Mick Jagger and Paul Simon), Gus G of Ozzy and many more.

To get more information about John McCarthy, his music and his instructional products visit RockHouseSchool.com.

## our roots

House of Blues is a home for live music and southern-inspired cuisine in an environment celebrating the African American cultural contributions to blues music and folk art. In 1992, our company converted an historical house in Cambridge, Massachusetts into the original House of Blues®. The original House of Blues opened its doors on Thanksgiving Day, 1992 feeding the homeless before opening to the public. Our commitment to serving the community will always be a priority.

We now have the pleasure of bringing live music to 16 major markets in the U. S. and Canada through our 10 club and 19 arena and amphitheatre venues. Come share the House of Blues experience. Get intimate with your favorite band in our Music Hall or enjoy soulful sounds and eats at our popular weekend Gospel Brunch. Savor down home, southern inspired cooking in the restaurant. Be a VIP for an exclusive night out in the membership club Foundation Room. Celebrate an important event in one of our cool private party rooms and take home a special souvenir from our retail store. We look forward to welcoming you to our house!

## our mission

To create a profitable, principled global entertainment company.
To celebrate the diversity and brotherhood of world culture.
To promote racial and spiritual harmony through love, peace, truth,
  righteousness and non-violence.

## musical diversity

In our Music Halls, you will find almost every music genre imaginable. Rock n' Roll, Punk, Alternative, Heavy Metal, Rap, Country, Hip-Hop, Rhythm and Blues, Rock en Español, Jazz, Zydeco, Folk, Electronica and many other genres grace our stages. We welcome and celebrate music as a form of art and expression.

Music is a celebration. We design and manage venues with the complete experience in mind. *Best Outdoor Venue. Theatre of the Year. Arena/Auditorium of the Year. Best Large Outdoor Concert Venue. Best Live Music Club of the Year. Talent Buyer of the Year.* From large amphitheatres and arenas to small clubs, our venues and staff garner industry accolades year after year. View our upcoming shows, buy tickets and register for presales and special offers at www.hob.com.

The Gorge Amphitheatre is located in George, WA and has been voted Best Outdoor Arena several years running.

## the visual blues

The House of Blues' walls feature American folk art affectionately referred to as the visual blues. With over a thousand original pieces of folk art, House of Blues houses one of the largest publicly displayed folk art collections in America. Like music, these pieces represent a form of artistic expression available to everyone.

## philanthropy

Throughout our support of the International House of Blues Foundation (IHOBF), over 50,000 students and teachers experience the Blues SchoolHouse program in our music halls annually. This program explores the history, music and cultural impact of the blues and related folk art through live music, narration and a guided tour of our folk art collection. The program highlights African American cultural contributions and emphasizes the importance of personal expression. The IHOBF is dedicated to promoting cultural understanding and creative expression through music and art (www.ihobf.org).

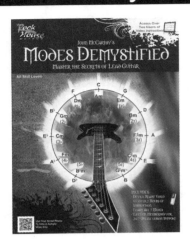
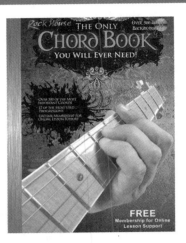